Ways of Knowing in Scienc

RICHARD DUSCHL, SERIES EDI'

I0469995

Transforming Middle School Science Education
Paul DeHart Hurd

Designing Project-Based Science: Connecting Learners
Through Guided Inquiry
Joseph L. Polman

Implementing Standards-Based Mathematics Instruction:
A Casebook for Professional Development
*Mary Kay Stein, Margaret Schwan Smith,
Marjorie A. Henningsen, and Edward A. Silver*

The New Science Teacher: Cultivating Good Practice
Deborah Trumbull

Problems of Meaning in Science Curriculum
Douglas A. Roberts and Leif Östman, Editors

Inventing Science Education for the New Millennium
Paul DeHart Hurd

Improving Teaching and Learning in Science and Mathematics
David F. Treagust, Reinders Duit, and Barry J. Fraser, Editors

Reforming Mathematics Education in America's Cities:
The Urban Mathematics Collaborative Project
Norman L. Webb and Thomas A. Romberg, Editors

What Children Bring to Light:
A Constructivist Perspective on Children's Learning in Science
Bonnie L. Shapiro

STS Education: International Perspectives on Reform
Joan Solomon and Glen Aikenhead, Editors

Reforming Science Education:
Social Perspectives and Personal Reflections
Rodger W. Bybee

Transforming Middle School Science Education

Paul DeHart Hurd

FOREWORD BY JAMES J. GALLAGHER

Teachers College, Columbia University
New York and London

Published by Teachers College Press, 1234 Amsterdam Avenue, New York, NY 10027

Library of Congress Cataloging-in-Publication Data

Hurd, Paul DeHart, 1905–
    Transforming middle school science education / Paul DeHart Hurd ; foreword by James J. Gallagher.
        p.   cm. — (Ways of knowing in science series)
    Includes bibliographical references and index.
    ISBN 0-8077-3923-5 (cloth : alk. paper) — ISBN 0-8077-3922-7 (pbk. : alk. paper)
        1. Science—Study and teaching (Middle School)—United States.
    2. Adolescence—United States.   3. Educational change—United States.   I. Title.
    II. Series.
    LB1585.3.H89   2000
    507.1'2—dc21   99-052996

ISBN 0-8077-3922-7 (paper)
ISBN 0-8077-3923-5 (cloth)

Printed on acid-free paper
Manufactured in the United States of America

07   06   05   04   03   02   01   00   8   7   6   5   4   3   2   1

For the twenty-one middle school dropouts who individually and in groups for a period of a week shared their views on schooling and life as we sat on the curb outside their school

Contents

Foreword

A hundred years have passed since it was first recognized that developing adolescents should receive an education in the sciences that meets their needs. Over the years dozens of middle grades curriculum reforms have taken place. . . . [T]hese science education reform movements have consistently remained . . . unconnected with life in the real world or with the adaptive needs of early adolescents.

The quote above marks the beginning of Chapter 7 of this book, Paul Hurd's new treatise on middle school science. In this work, Professor Hurd does again what he has done so well in previous writings—he provides us with a comprehensive summary of the vast literature on this topic that has both historical perspective and the most current research and scholarship. He then goes on to weave a soundly logical, visionary proposal for remaking science for middle school students, which is consistent with and supported by the work and wisdom of many diverse thinkers on the topic.

In the first six chapters of this book, Paul Hurd catalogs study after study that convincingly point to the need for a curriculum in science for early adolescents that addresses their personal, social, developmental, and emotional needs. He cites the staggering statistics on the numbers of youth who are in various kinds of "trouble" that lead to isolation, antisocial behavior, and even self-destruction. To these facts he holds a mirror that reflects how program after program for youth has focused on the disciplines of science while "forgetting" adolescent students. Yet program proponents claim that they are "meeting students' needs."

In Chapter 7, Professor Hurd then proposes a "living curriculum" for middle school science designed to meet the adaptive needs of students for life and living in the new information age. He states that this "living curriculum" is:

- In harmony with the new paradigm of science
- Personally, socially, culturally, and economically oriented to the needs of both adolescents and our transforming society

- Interdisciplinary in nature
- Directed to aiding students to make sense of science in everyday life and viewed as active knowledge to be experienced by students
- Fluid and capable of responding to new developments within science or society
- An instrument of service for dealing with life and living

Chapter 8 adds an important dimension to the curriculum—human health. Hurd argues convincingly for helping students learn science through this very personal perspective. He also cites an array of studies conducted over the past decade to support this position. In Chapter 9 he identifies criteria for selection of subject matter for middle school science and then sketches in moderate detail one way to organize the content of the "living curriculum" as a three-year program.

In the closing chapter of this work, Professor Hurd reminds us of the complexity of the task before us and of the need for new ways of meeting it. He quotes Einstein, who admonished colleagues by saying that "you cannot solve a problem by thinking in the same terms that caused the problem." In this book, Hurd shows his scholarship and creativity in presenting to us the knowledge of decades of study and reflection by many diverse thinkers about the problems of educating early adolescents. He tells a compelling story about the needs of these young people and then offers a challenging plan to address these needs.

This work should be provocative of debate and action for all who have a responsibility to educate adolescents. It carries a strong message, not only for those of us who are interested in education about science, but also for all who work with middle grades students.

This book serves another function, beyond that of framing a new vision for people who work with middle grades students. It is also a model of the kind of interdisciplinary scholarship that is needed in our field. For more than half a century, Paul Hurd has been exemplary in applying this broad, creative, integrating scholarship in the field of science education. Few have followed his example; more in our field should.

The many lessons in this book are of great importance. It should be read with thoughtfulness, then followed by action!

James J. Gallagher
Professor of Science Education, Michigan State University

Preface

The current reform movement in science education has been underway since the early 1970s. During this period it has become increasingly clear that today's world is undergoing revolutionary changes to which adolescents must adapt. There are transitions into a knowledge-intensive society, a global economy, and changes in the culture and practice of the sciences. Since midcentury, major shifts have also taken place in family structures and in how people live, work, and learn. We now live in a learning society where knowledge is the chief measure of human capital.

Numerous proposals have been formulated for bringing science education into harmony with this new age of ours and its forseeable future. Overlooked in this process until recently has been the significance of these changes in the development and adaptation of the early adolescent. Today, the most critical educational reformers view the middle grades science curriculum as a "fraud" and a "cognitive swindle" in terms of preparing students for their lifeworld.

Nowhere do we find the early adolescent at the center of science curricula in the middle years. A recognition of this problem is found in the slogans used to describe today's early adolescent, such as an "endangered species," an "imperiled generation," "growing up forgotten," "caught in the middle," "misguided and at risk," "roleless in our society," "products of an educational wasteland," and "an abandoned generation."

The education of the early adolescent has always been a problem. More than 2,000 years ago, Aristotle commented:

> The young are in character prone to desire and ready to carry any desire they may have formed into action. Of bodily desires it is the sexual to which they are most disposed to give way, and in regard to sexual desire they exercise no self-restraint. They are changeful too, and fickle in their desires, which are as transitory as they are vehement; for their wishes are keen without being permanent, like a sick man's fits of hunger and thirst. (quoted in Kiell, 1964)

In the United States, as early as 1649, the "uncivil carriage" of Massachusetts youth and their escape from parental government were noted in Middlesex court records; and in the 1680s, Cotton Mather, the clergyman and author, called for the formation of "Associations of Young Folks to direct the energy of youth into positive channels" (Langemann, 1993).

The task now before us as parents, teachers, and educators is to acknowledge that after 2,000 years we have yet to develop a middle grades curriculum that is focused on the biological, social, psychological, emotional, and cultural needs of the early adolescent. Nor do we have middle school science curricula that are supportive of emerging national goals that reflect the nation's movement from one era to that of the new millennium. The changed circumstances for adolescent development today call for equally great changes in the education they receive. This book is focused on inventing a science curriculum that is able to meet the needs of early adolescents in ways that are attuned to the nature of today's society and the practice and culture of science/technology.

In order for the needs of early adolescents to be met, the first task is to identify the maladjustive behaviors of today's adolescents. This approach is in contrast to the traditional method of reforming science curricula by simply updating the subject matter based on new discoveries in a discipline.

The author's view throughout this book is that the invention of new science curricula for the middle school begins with a study of adolescents, including their social behavior, biological characteristics, physical and emotional health, and other conditions that influence the student's life pattern. All of these attributes have roots in modern science.

The educational tone of this book is influenced by oral interviews with 121 middle grades science teachers and nearly two dozen middle school student dropouts.

1

Seeking to Understand
the Developing Adolescent

We know less about early adolescence than we ought to.
                                              —*Daedalus*

National efforts to reform education in the sciences have focused on the middle grades as needing the most attention. These grades coincide with the most crucial period in adolescent development. Currently the early adolescent in the United States is viewed as the least understood age group in our society. It is apparent that we need a clearer vision of what the middle school science curriculum should be about.

Today's science curricula are based on a perceived notion of the "structure of a science" and its "mode of inquiry" (American Association for the Advancement of Science, 1993; National Research Council, 1996a, 1996b). We need to recognize that adolescents are the primary source of data to guide the reform of curricula that are designed to meet their life needs in a changing society and economy.

The first two chapters of this book are devoted to a better understanding of today's early adolescents and the life problems they will face. A similar treatment of these problems is found in other studies (Feldman & Elliott, 1990; Takanishi, 1993). This present chapter is centered on getting to know something of today's adolescent and implications for the teaching of science. Historically science curricula reformers have tended to create programs disconnected from the biological, social, cultural and psychological characteristics of human beings. Yet educators throughout this century have prefaced their curriculum reform efforts with the statement "to meet the needs of students" without there being a study of what these needs might be. Efforts today to set national standards for science achievement in the middle grades portray a curriculum that is again isolated from students and the social and cultural environments to which they must adapt.

1

DEFINING AN ADOLESCENT

Adolescence as a state in human development that lies somewhere between childhood and adulthood is less clearly defined than is infancy, adulthood, or old age. Historically the concept of adolescence has changed far more profoundly than that of other age groups. The changes are biological as well as social and psychological. The age of biological maturity, puberty, occurs increasingly earlier in the United States, influenced by improved nutritional and health conditions. From another perspective, adolescence is a process of preparing oneself for adulthood by experimenting, studying, making choices, and resisting.

Problems associated with growing up have been particularly stressful during the past one hundred years, brought about by the nation's movement from an agricultural to an industrial society. Families moved from farms to cities, and developing adolescents became roleless in the family. By the 1900s large numbers of young adolescents sought to resolve their problems by joining gangs, using drugs and alcohol, and exhibiting other risky behaviors.

The onset of today's knowledge-intensive age, a global economy, new modes of communication and ways of working, the socialization of science, and changes in family structures have complicated the adaptive needs of early adolescents as they move from childhood to the next phase of maturity. Unfortunately, family and school expectations for the 11 to 14 age group remain those of past generations. Throughout this century an accepted view of adolescence has been that of a phase of human development characterized by "storm and stress," "upheaval and trauma," corresponding to humankind's evolutionary progress from savagery to civilization. Many parents hold the view that the only thing normal about an adolescent is abnormality. Currently this view is shifting from one that sees youths as brash and troublesome to one that sees them as vulnerable and in serious need of help.

Emerging adolescents describe their own feelings as "lonesomeness" and "nobody seems to care." Overall there is little argument that growing up today is harder than in past generations—the path is more obscure, choices are more difficult, and there is little help, especially from school curricula. In a personal discussion in the 1950s on problems of early adolescents, Margaret Mead, the renowned anthropologist, commented that changes in family structures with grandparents moving away to live on their own have removed the only shoulder that early adolescents can cry on.

There is a dearth of longitudinal studies that might provide perspective for dealing with current problems of adolescent development and adaptation. What has emerged during today's educational reform movement is that the middle/junior high school years are the most critical and the greatest in need of reconceptualization and restructuring. And in the matrix of reform, science teaching is perceived as requiring the greatest attention, primarily because both the cultural context and the practice of today's science are different from those of the past.

EARLY ADOLESCENT AND PUBERTY PROCESSES

From childhood to adulthood there is a range of life changes to which young persons must adapt. These changes fall broadly into the biological and social spheres. Biological changes include bodily and sexual developments. Over a period of several years a child must negotiate sexual arousal, awareness of the opposite sex, sexual experiences, and decisions about contraceptives. The meaning of these reproductive events is influenced by (a) culturally mediated beliefs, (b) parental interactive patterns, and (c) personality characteristics and other factors such as school transitions, self-esteem, peer relations, and sense of attractiveness. Besides the biological, environmental, and social factors influencing development, there is an array of life events including the tempo of social changes, race, family behaviors, and religion. The main constant in adolescent development is progress toward a capacity for reproduction. Changes during puberty are influenced by hormonal factors, genetics, nutrition, presence or absence of disease, and ethnic factors as well as the rate of development. Growth spurts differ for boys and girls.

Puberty elicits a wide array of emotions on the part of individuals; they may feel alternately excited or scared, pleased or distraught, and given the rapidity with which these changes occur, they may experience bewilderment. The first menstrual period (menarche) influences a girl's sense of social security, peer prestige, self-consciousness, and self-esteem and produces a heightened awareness of her body. Girls unprepared for menarche have more negative reactions than those who were prepared for the event.

Late maturity for boys is a particular disadvantage with respect to self-esteem, popularity, and "macho" behavior. Early maturing girls have a smaller network of girlfriends and poorer emotional habits. Both early maturing boys and girls are more likely to engage in adult behaviors, such as smoking, drinking, and intercourse, at a younger age than on-time or late maturers.

Adolescents are concerned about their current and future appearance. Girls are particularly sensitive about their weight and have a desire to be thin. A study of normal-weight girls found that nearly two thirds rated themselves as overweight. For boys the major concern is engagement in athletic events. For both boys and girls, when expectations do not match future realities, risky behaviors are likely to appear.

Puberty processes influence the emotional health of early adolescents. Common effects are depression and conduct disorders. Six percent of early adolescents have severe emotional problems (Holmes, Kaplan, Lang, & Card, 1991). Conduct disorders such as aggressiveness and violence are more common in boys. Girls develop two years earlier than boys, and some boys develop before other boys of the same age (Tanner, 1971, pp. 909–930). Boys tend to have a bigger circle of friends during puberty development than do girls. Girls talk with their parents about problems more frequently than boys do. Parents expect increasing adult behaviors throughout puberty.

Developmental factors during puberty have educational implications. The transition from elementary to middle school is particularly stressful, often serving to lower self-esteem, which in turn lowers school achievement. Education in sex and family life are best started at the fifth or sixth grade at the latest. Efforts to assure the self-esteem of young adolescents are essential. Pressures for adultlike behavior on the part of adolescents need to be minimized by teachers and parents.

There is much more to learn about adolescent development. Biological factors are better understood than the social forces. The old notion that adolescence is simply a period of storm and stress to be endured or tolerated is no longer a perspective accepted by researchers on adolescent development.

THE ADOLESCENT SELF—THE STRUGGLE FOR IDENTITY

Studies of self in adolescence are focused on the development of self-esteem and on fluctuations in self-concept. Entrance into adolescence brings about a dramatic shift toward introspection, when one turns to self as an object of observation and reflection, seeking to answer the question, *Who am I?* In my interviews with urban junior high school dropouts about the reasons for leaving school, their most frequent responses were "they don't tell you anything about yourself" and "they don't tell you anything about other kids." It takes little effort to validate these comments through an examination of the middle grades curriculum (Hurd, 1998).

The biology courses offered in middle schools could deal with concepts of human behavior and adaptation, but they do not. From the standpoint of schooling, more attention is required in helping each adolescent develop a sense of worth as a person and how to enhance it throughout life. The ground rules for the foreseeable future are different from those of past generations.

MALADAPTIVE DECISIONS OF TODAY'S ADOLESCENTS

Today, early adolescents of 12 to 14 years of age are facing an array of social, economic, family, and biological changes to which they must adapt. There are 19 million children in this age group. They are growing up in a new era in the nation's history, a period of rapid change. They have little guidance for meeting the life problems they encounter. Consequently they make a host of risky and fateful choices (Hechinger, 1992; Takanishi, 1993). For example, two thirds of this age group have tried alcohol; a third have tried illicit drugs; the percentage with AIDS and other sexually transmitted diseases is increasing. "The consumption of alcohol leads to risky sexual behavior such as unprotected intercourse and a likelihood of AIDS" (Kleiman, 1998, pp. 47–52). A recent study of drug habits in eighth graders revealed that 26.2% used alcohol and 15% engaged in binge drinking. In addition, it was found that 11.3% of eighth graders used marijuana, 5.8% used inhalants, and 1.3% used cocaine (National Center for Health Statistics, 1996). By age 14, 23% of early adolescents report that they have had sexual intercourse (Guttmacher Institute, 1994, p. 19). Suicide rates have almost tripled since 1968 and about a third of early adolescents experience serious depression.

Today's early adolescents have less interaction with parents; nearly half will at some time live in a home with a single parent. In the majority of homes, both parents work and for three or more hours per day no parent is home. It is in this period that many early adolescents experiment with alcohol, drugs, and sex, whereas others watch television (Moore, 1992).

EARLY ADOLESCENT HEALTH

The behavioral view of health is not about diseases, it is related to preventable social, environmental, and behavioral factors, such as accidents, homicide, and suicide; to causes of morbidity, including disabilities; and to the consequences of sexual activities (early pregnancy, abortion, and substance abuse). These social and behavioral factors are viewed in the context of total health throughout one's lifetime. The relationship between behavioral factors and health status is well documented.

Adolescent health status as presently recognized by adults is greatly overestimated. Data on adolescent health are based primarily on the utilization of medical services such as hospital discharge rates and on conditions cited in visits to office-based physicians, police reports on accidents, homicide, and suicide. Young people in the most need of medical care, the inner-city youth, the poor, and new immigrants, are not reflected in the statistical data on health needs. One in five early adolescents live in poverty and receive little medical attention except for serious accidents (Lipsitz, 1991). Between early (ages 10–14) and late (ages 15–19) adolescence, mortality rates shift by more than 200% due largely to violent causes of death. The increased rate for motor vehicle accidents and homicide is 400% and for suicide 600%. Top-ranked cause of death for African American youths is homicide and for Whites suicide, and the combined rates are twice as high for males as for females. Unrecognized in these data are health worries, such as menstrual problems, acne, dental conditions, depression, and nervousness. "In the past 20 years the number of obese children has doubled placing more Americans at risk" for an array of health and emotional problems (Glickman, 1998, 11-A).

If we consider a concept of wellness as more than simply the absence of disease or illness, most developing adolescents are vastly underserved. Adolescents visit private physicians at a lower rate than any other age group. Comprehensive estimates of the number of adolescents who receive no regular health care are difficult to obtain. Sample studies indicate the number is between 40 and 50% depending in part on the community in which these adolescents live. Health care systems are particularly lacking in the psychological and reproductive areas. Nationwide, 20.5% of early adolescents have seriously considered suicide, 15.7% made a suicide plan, 7.7% attempted suicide, and 2.6% required medical attention because of a suicide attempt (U.S. Bureau of the Census, 1993; Gallup International Institute, 1991).

Proper timing for health care education is in the middle grades. Such programs should focus on both the psychosocial and biological parameters. Although the middle grades coincide with entrance into puberty, there is little health education.

EARLY ADOLESCENT SEXUAL BEHAVIOR

"Reproductive maturation is the most distinctive feature of the transition from childhood to adulthood" (Katchadourian, 1990, p. 330). Traditionally society, including parents, has tended to suppress, ignore, or weakly influence the sexual behavior of adolescents. While the process of sexual development is mostly biological, it also has social and cultural contexts. Forces influencing today's developing adolescents vary from those of previous generations.

Parents view sexual experiences in teenagers as different from their own. Whatever the realities of sexual activities in young adolescents, they tend to get blown out of all proportion on the one hand, while on the other hand there exists a feeling that sexual problems in adolescents are natural and must be accepted—so why worry? The spread of AIDS into the adolescent population has served to stimulate public support for sex education in schools. Between 1960–1988, gonorrhea increased fourfold among 10- to 14-year-olds. The teen pregnancy rate increased 23% from 1973 to 1987 (Hechinger, 1992, chap. 1).

The importance of peer influences on sexual development of adolescents, like the influence of the family, is taken for granted. Peer and parent influences tend to complement each other, though less so in periods of social change when generational values change. At these times peer influence takes precedence. The extent of influences varies with gender and ethnic background. "Every year in America about 560,000 teenagers give birth. Most are unmarried and a majority are not ready for the emotional, psychological, and financial responsibilities and challenges of parenthood. Teenage childbearing has important health and social consequences for the young women, their babies, and their families" (Ventura et al., 1997). The teenage birth rate has been on the decline in the 1990s, due largely to the widespread use of contraceptives and fear of contracting AIDS. The number of teenage abortions and fetal statistics are not known. Of every 1,000 births per year in the United States 1.4 births are to mothers 10–14 years of age (Daley, 1997, p. 75).

PEER GROUPS AND GANGS

In the eyes of many teachers and parents, adolescents seem to have a passionate herding instinct. They form groups, they spend hours telephoning friends, and they go in packs to shopping malls and other places. Peer groups are a significant part of adolescent behavior and development. Much is said and written about peer groups, especially gangs and the impact they have on creating uniformity and single-mindedness among young people. However, there are multiple peer cultures that encourage diversity in value systems and behavior.

There is little evidence that peer pressures overpower the values of parents. Where conflicting advice is offered to adolescents, they tend to discriminate in choice of advice. There is a strong congruence of values between those held by parents and those portrayed by the developing adolescent. When adolescents accept peer norms that are in opposition to adult norms, it is likely that they were "pushed" into the behavior by hostile child-raising practices rather than by being "pulled" into the peer group. We need to abandon the notion that youths are united into a general culture that stands in opposition to adult society.

Peer systems in the middle grades are not uniquely different from cliquish practices of the elementary school or the larger network of peer relations at the high school age. At all age levels participation in a peer group represents some measure of an individual's social skills. It is within a peer group that the adolescent seeks identity, develops friends, and learns how to fit into a crowd. These groups provide a place where a developing adolescent can try out various identities.

However we view peer groups, cliques, and gangs, they serve as an important factor in negotiating adolescence. Teenagers must always struggle with the tension between having no group identification versus having a peer affiliation, even to the point of being in a group they dislike. As children mature they become increasingly sensitive to their place in the crowd: which peer groups will include them and which will exclude them, as well as membership in any peer system, especially if it is viewed as "freakish." Not all crowds are equally receptive to new members. How adults influence or intervene in the peer system is typically not systematic. Schools influence peer groups by emphasizing academic achievement, supporting social clubs, and favoring sports and music. Each of these groups generates different social skills in its members.

Research findings indicate that though adolescents are inclined to accede to peer influence, peer pressure does not seem to wholly dictate adolescent behavior. Susceptibility to peer pressure varies among adolescents exposed to different family structures and parenting styles. Furthermore, in one way or another, for better or worse, adults and schools intervene in teenage peer cultures. For example, the relative emphasis a school staff gives to sports, academic, and particular extracurricular activities is likely to define the types of crowds that emerge in a school.

FRIENDS ARE IMPORTANT TO ADOLESCENTS

In childhood, parents and other adults are central to a child's development. At entrance into adolescence it is peer friendships that influence and support the development of the individual. In Western societies, success in forming and maintaining peer relations is an indicator of social and psychological adjustment. The importance of peer friendships is reflected in the amount of time that adolescents spend with friends; during the course of adolescence, time with friends increases and that with parents decreases.

To adolescents, a friend is one who is loyal and "doesn't talk about you behind your back." Having friends provides opportunities to share thoughts and experiences, especially intimate thoughts. This sense of intimacy is critically significant in friendships, more so for girls than for boys. For both sexes it is through friends that one develops a sense of identity and place in society. Adolescents typically report that they enjoy their activities with friends more than any other activity. With friends adolescents feel as if they can be understood and can become fully themselves. Unpopular, neglected, and rejected adolescents with few or no friends are likely to be aggressive, to drop out of school, to engage in criminal behavior, or to develop a mental illness.

Public opinion polls tend to show support for sex education in the middle grades. Adolescents themselves feel it should be a part of their education. Where middle school courses have been developed, the topics typically cover reproductive sexual anatomy, the physical and psychological changes in puberty, and sexually transmitted diseases. Most sex education programs are short (10 hours or less), and are simply an added-on topic to biology, health, or physical education courses.

Another variety of peer relationships is romance. By the middle grades, other-sex friendships increase, especially among girls, although they never constitute the majority of best-friend relations. Girl's relationships are usually with older boys who are from another school. In general, opposite-sex relationships in the middle grades represent "dating opportunities" more than legitimate friendships.

The influence of friends extends beyond concerns of immediate relevance such as clothes, entertainment, and companionship to include social behaviors, attitudes, and beliefs that have important consequences for adolescents and their society. For example, friends influence educational aspirations, the use of alcohol, and substance abuse. Parents as well as friends influence the use of alcohol and tobacco; three fourths of the adolescents who smoke have at least one member of their family who also smokes. The influence of an adolescent's friends on one's behavior is magnified when adolescents perceive their parental relationship as negative, such as parents not liking them, or not providing any kind of guidance. Overall, parents appear to exert a greater influence than the best friend in terms of educational plans.

The extent of friend influence is likely to be greater if the friendship is stable, reciprocated, and exclusive. If an adolescent has many friends,

the power of any one friend is less than if he or she were the only confi-
dant of the adolescent. What the influence is likely to be is often domain
specific, for example, one may influence dress, whereas another will influence sport participation. On the whole, writers who lament or praise
the effects of friends on adolescents' behavior say almost nothing about
how this influence or power is applied or why it is effective. Furthermore, no single context encompasses the multiple forms that peer influence has on adolescent behavior. Even when friends do not exert pressure, adolescents are likely to conform, because they want to be accepted
by their friends and because they admire individuals who live up to the
group's norm.

There is clear evidence that close peer relations are desirable during
adolescence. Friends seek mutual understanding, openness, trust, and
acceptance within this relationship and life problems are worked out.
One discovers in friendship one's unique place in the world. Around the
age of 15 about a third of adolescents engage in work in addition to
schooling. Students who work develop new peer groups and are more
likely to drop out of school and to use alcohol and drugs (Guttmacher
Institute, 1994).

STRESS AND COPING

Significant causes of early adolescent stress are death in the family, divorce, or having only a single parent. Adopted adolescents report a
higher level of risk behaviors than those not adopted (Benson, Sharma, &
Roenlkepartain, 1994, p. 105). Emerging adolescents typically resent re-
marriage of a parent in the case of divorce. Boys are more negatively
influenced by changes in family structure than are girls. How signifi-
cantly early adolescents are influenced by the breakup of a family involves the extent of hostility within the family before separation and the
support system afterwards. The last factor includes the attitude friends
take to the changed situation. Only 40% of children who start school
with a full family will be in the same structure by the time they graduate
from high school, and the earlier in the student's life that family dissolu-
tion takes place the greater the degree of stress. In 1994, 30.8% of families
consisted of one parent; 26.6% were headed by the mother and 4.2% by
the father (U.S. Bureau of the Census, 1994).

A common outcome of the inability to cope with life's problems is
suicide. Between the ages of 15 and 24 it is the second leading cause of
death. Whereas the problems of attempted suicide and suicide previously began in the high school years, the percentage is now increasing

in the middle school years. Early warning signs include conduct disorders, drug or alcohol use (in 70% of suicide cases), loss of self-esteem (65% of instances), depression, and changes within the nuclear family (Gallup International Institute, 1991, p. 75; U.S. Bureau of the Census, 1993, p. 99). Other warning signs may be changes in appetite and sleep patterns, decreased concentration, social withdrawal, and a loss of interest in usual activities.

SUMMARY

Of the 19 million early adolescents in the United States, three out of four engage in little or no risky behavior, and the remaining one in four are in significant trouble. The Children's Defense Fund prepares an annual list of youth problems called "Every Day in America." The youth list for 1996 gives the *daily* toll as follows: "[Three] died from abuse or neglect; 6 committed suicide; 16 were killed with guns; 316 were arrested for violent crimes; 406 were arrested for drug offenses; 466 babies were born to mothers who had little or no prenatal healthcare; 1,420 babies were born to teenagers; 2,556 babies were born into poverty; 3,533 were born to unwed mothers; 3,356 dropped out of high school; 5,702 were arrested; 13,076 were suspended from school; and 100,000 remain homeless" (National Issues Forums, 1997, p. 2).

It is these and related observations of early adolescents that have led teachers and educators to express a need for a middle school with special curricula that can serve to close the gaps between early adolescents and their well-being. Various aspects of this problem are the subject of the chapters that comprise this book.

2

At the Crossroads

STRESS AND COPING IN YOUNG ADOLESCENCE

The transition through adolescence is seldom smooth, but about 80% of children are able to handle the varied stresses and challenges without unusual duress. The 20% who have difficulty make up about the same percentage as of adults who have adjustment and adaptation problems.

The study of stress, coping, and adaptation in early adolescence is receiving increased attention from researchers. Efforts are being made to reconceptualize this field of study and to find ways of relating social, biological, and psychological factors within the middle school curriculum.

Coping is the process by which individuals respond to and manage stress. The concept includes the making of decisions to resolve a problem without creating risk. Unfortunately there is little in the middle school curriculum designed to guide these decisions in a favorable way.

MOTIVATION AND ACADEMIC ACHIEVEMENT
IN EARLY ADOLESCENCE

As the adolescent develops, the pattern of social and academic pressures changes. Academic achievement has been found to be more influenced by psychological factors, such as teachers who listen and encourage achievement, than by simply a student's intellectual ability. A student who is less bright but is highly motivated is more likely to be a high achiever than a bright student who gets little attention or encouragement.

Gender influences academic achievement. In the elementary school, girls tend to get better grades than boys, especially in verbal subjects. In the middle school years girls perform less well than boys in the sciences and boys less well in languages and history. These results are the products of teaching procedures rather than natural ability.

12

SCHOOLS AND THE EARLY ADOLESCENT

There is little research that bears directly on how the schools affect various aspects of adolescent development. For example, there are no controlled studies that demonstrate whether a K–8, 6-7-8, or 7-8-9 grade organization is the most favorable for adolescent development. The current movement toward a middle school structure is based on intuition and experience in working with adolescents. Nor is it possible to sharply distinguish between the influences of school, home, church, or environmental factors on how children progress through adolescence. Large-scale quantitative studies, however, do provide clues about the influence of schools on development. For example, schools that are smaller in enrollment, that have a variety of social activities, that have a large, cooperative parent clientele, and where teachers call children by their first names make for a favorable social environment for developing adolescents. Participation in extracurricular activities correlates positively with academic performance, perhaps because such activities link students to the larger society of the school, especially the teachers.

Academic performances of middle grade students have been found to be influenced by ethnic factors. Asians typically perform better than Whites, African Americans and Hispanics less well. Participation in athletics neither depresses nor especially enhances academic performance. Differences in family structure, socioeconomic background, and demographic location have been shown to influence student achievement. There is a consensus that adolescent subcultures or peer groups influence student achievement. Furthermore, there is a positive correlation between student achievement and teacher certification, holding of advanced degrees, and years of experience (Hurd, 1999). However, teachers' actions and attitudes displayed in the classroom do matter, exhibited in such factors as high expectations for students, class organization, and homework that is corrected.

The findings from studies of ability grouping or tracking are mixed. Tracking is seen as a negative influence on the development of the early adolescent's self-esteem and social relations. Research on desegregation consistently reports weak or uncertain results in achievement. Tracking and holding students back a grade or so leads to greater school absenteeism, an increased drop-out rate, and a lowering of self-esteem.

The transition from an elementary to a middle or junior high school creates problems of stress in the developing adolescent because of differences in how schools and classes are organized and the increased size of school enrollment. The change in social roles tends to lower self-esteem as one seeks a new peer group and friends. White females seem to be most affected by a loss of self-esteem. Reports from students indicate that stress factors from entrance into a middle or junior high school arise from various conditions: Teachers care less about students and are not friendly, teachers grade less fairly than in elementary school, fewer opportunities to interact with teachers exist, and classwork is more rigorous. These student perceptions occur at just the age when their self-images are the most fragile. Also, parents take less interest in middle school affairs than in those of the elementary school.

EARLY ADOLESCENTS AND THEIR USE OF LEISURE

Adolescents say that one of their major problems is "lonesomeness." It is only in recent years that studies have been carried out on what leisure means to the adolescent and how it is used. Leisure preferences and behaviors are somewhat different for boys and girls and for members of different races, ethnic groups, and social classes. Excluding sleep, early adolescents spend 40% of their time on leisure activities (sports, games, socializing); 29% of their time on schooling and working activities; and 31% of their time on maintenance activities (sleeping and eating). More than half (68%) read a newspaper and 58% a magazine. On the average, early adolescents spend 22 hours per week watching television (Batezel, 1968; Johnson, 1994). By the time they reach 18, adolescents as a group will have spent more hours in front of television sets than in classrooms. During their viewing time, the average early adolescent will see about 1,000 murders, rapes, or aggravated assaults each year (Abelson, 1995).

Most leisure activities take place in the adolescent "social world"; sports, games, and listening to music are the most common areas. The sphere of adolescent action, usually described as "just hanging out together," is mostly shared with peers. The location or territory for "hanging out" has moved from the street corner to the mall in recent years. Gangs describe the place to hang out as their territory, which to the early adolescent is as important as the activity carried on there.

The closest thing to a distinctive leisure activity that is apparent in most adolescents' lives is music. The popular music enjoyed by adolescents is the major support for recording companies and adolescents their chief market.

Leisure is a part of the socializing experiences of the adolescent. How they spend their time provides opportunities for adolescents to structure their own lives and brings them into an accommodation outside the home. Extracurricular activities in the middle grades not only provide the student with leisure choices, but also correlate positively with academic achievement and interest in schoolwork. There is a need for middle schools to take a greater interest in developing leisure programs for students, especially activities in which adolescents can share in the planning.

THE EARLY ADOLESCENT AND MASS MEDIA

Currently the revolutionary changes in the management of information through Internet links and the World Wide Web are beginning to influence how early adolescents use their time for both learning and recreation. There is no doubt that Internet links and the World Wide Web will change the character of early adolescents development in more ways than we can now imagine (Cohen, 1997). We do know that computers fascinate the early adolescent both as a mode of learning and as entertainment.

DELINQUENT OR DEVIANT BEHAVIORS
IN EARLY ADOLESCENCE

Early adolescent behavior that breaks the norms of childhood is considered "deviant" or "delinquent"; such behavior includes drug and alcohol use and street crimes. Between the ages of 11 and 17, 7 to 8% of boys and 3.5% of girls have a record of delinquency (Whitaker & Bastian, 1991, p. 13).

Efforts to find explanations for deviant behavior focus on social injustice (lack of legitimate opportunities for success), parental inadequacies, biogenetic susceptibilities, personality and character traits, and vulnerability to peer influences. Frustrating school experiences tend to promote deviant behavior. Drug use and adolescent crime tend to thrive among those who have few opportunities to reap benefits from conformity.

NEXT STEPS

Chapters 1 and 2 provide a first step in a road map for science curriculum developments designed to meet the needs of today's early adolescents. While this goal has been emphasized for the past 100 years by teachers and educators, there have been little supportive curricula. Now for the first time in the history of middle grades science education, the reform movement in science teaching is focused on various dimensions of today's adolescent growth and development, including the biological, behavioral, physical, and social characteristics—real life. It is within this context that science education standards are sought. Currently, the move is to foster science curriculum standards in terms of their meaning for understanding oneself, attaining a high quality of life, and developing human capital, rather than understanding the structure of science disciplines.

NOTE

Data on the risk behaviors of early adolescents are in the process of being restudied using a new approach. The new technique is known as Audio-CASI technology; students respond to questions they have been asked by using headphones and pressing numbered keys on a computer keyboard. Respondents can thus answer questions in complete privacy, even if their reading ability is limited. In using this approach researchers found that adolescent risk behaviors were higher by a factor of 3 or more compared to student responses to an interviewer or a written questionnaire. For example, 5.3% of boys admitted to male-male sex behavior using the Audio-CASI technique as compared to 1.8% on a paper questionnaire. Other examples: using a needle to take street drugs—6.1% (paper) vs. 8.7% (Audio-CASI); drinking alcohol weekly—15% (paper) vs. 19.4% (Audio-CASI). The researchers conclude that "overall the risks adolescents are taking today are substantially greater than was previously supposed" (Turner et al., 1998).

3

Issues in Educating Developing Adolescents

Traditionally, the school setting for educating the early adolescent has been the eight-grade elementary school and a 4-year high school. Some concern has always prevailed that this arrangement was not the best for the education of developing adolescents, who are neither children nor adults. In 1892 Charles W. Eliot, president of Harvard University, proposed to the National Education Association the development of a 6-year elementary plus a 6-year secondary school organization. Eliot's principal concern was the quality of a student's preparation for entering the university. There is no record of schools adopting this grade arrangement.

Problems with the schooling of early adolescents in the early 1900s gained attention when the pupil school dropout rate reached a high of 65% (Ayres, 1909; Thorndike, 1907). It was at this time that the nation was moving from being an agricultural to being an industrial society. Rural families were moving from the farm to cities and a new way of life. Many early adolescents were finding it difficult to adapt to the new life conditions. Violence, drugs, and alcohol addiction were their solutions to life problems. G. Stanley Hall, the originator of adolescent psychology, was the first to recognize that developing adolescents are different from children and mature adults. He implied the need for special schools where early adolescents could be isolated and educated in special ways.

Changes in school organization specifically to accommodate the early adolescent were initiated in 1909 in Berkeley, California, and Columbus, Ohio. These schools took the form of segregating grades 7, 8, and 9 into a separate school, generally labeled a junior high school or intermediate school.

Over the following 30 years, numerous reports, articles, and studies were published in hopes of providing a rationale for junior high school education (Briggs, 1927; Douglass, 1916; Koos, 1920). In 1940, W. T. Gruhn and H. R. Douglas developed a synthesis of writings on the rationale and functions of junior high education covering the period from 1910 to 1940. In 1970 they redid the 1940 synthesis to reflect more recent thinking on the educational functions of the junior high school (Gruhn & Douglas, 1971). There is little difference between the two statements; a summary of the 1970 version on the functions of the junior high school follows:

1. *Integration.* To provide learning experiences that can be integrated into effective and wholesome pupil behavior as well as provide for a correlation between subjects in the curriculum
2. *Exploration.* To lead pupils to discover and explore their own interests, abilities, and skills and to provide opportunities to include cultural, social, civic, avocational, and recreational interests as a basis for vocational decision
3. *Guidance.* To assist pupils in making intelligent decisions about their education and vocational choices and to make wholesome social and personal decisions
4. *Differentiation.* To provide educational opportunities for pupils of different backgrounds, interests, abilities, and needs
5. *Socialization.* To provide learning experiences that will enable pupils as citizens to participate in and contribute to our democratic society
6. *Articulation.* To help pupils acquire the backgrounds and skills that will help them succeed in the secondary school, post-secondary schools, and adult life

In 1960, 50 years after the origin of junior high schools, educators recognized that the ideal functions of the junior high school were not being attained. The word "junior" came to mean a scaled-down version of its "senior" counterpart. This condition extended to the curriculum, textbooks, instructional practices, varsity athletic teams, and social activities such as proms and formal dances (Conant, 1960; Educational Research Council of Greater Cleveland, 1960; Grambs, Noyce, Patterson, & Robertson, 1961; National Association of Secondary School Principals, 1960).

The vision of an effective school for early adolescents has been dulled by a series of continuing problems. The lack of qualified teachers in the junior high school has always been a central problem. Typically, teachers in junior high schools have been educated as elementary or senior high school teachers. Those trained as high school teachers have the most difficulty adjusting to a junior high school assignment. Perceived pressures from scholastic achievement tests and college entrance requirements, and the need to specify ninth-grade courses in terms of separate subjects have led to a questioning of the junior high school as the proper administrative unit for achieving the ideal education of early adolescents.

The issue was brought into focus during the late 1950s and early 1960s in a wave of criticism of all precollege education (Goodman, 1964; Hart, 1969; Hentoff, 1967; Holt, 1964; Kozol, 1967; Rockefeller Brothers Fund, 1958; Silberman, 1970). In response to the criticisms of the junior high school and the call for new directions in American education, William Alexander proposed the development of a "middle school," a name commonly used in European schools for early adolescents. He and others began the conceptualization of what a middle school should mean (Alexander, 1964; Alexander & Williams, 1965; Alexander, Williams, Comptom, Hines, & Prescott, 1968). In summary, the ideal middle school was viewed as (a) focusing on the needs of early adolescents, (b) providing individualized instruction, (c) stressing the intellectual components of a curriculum, (d) emphasizing inquiry, discovery, and learning how to learn, (e) providing many exploratory experiences, (f) offering health and physical education programs appropriate to the age group, (g) placing an emphasis on values throughout all courses, and (h) educating teachers in the special competencies needed to work effectively with the early adolescent. These attributes were influenced by the research of Jean Piaget and J. M. Tanner on the intellectual and physical development of early adolescents (e.g., Inhelder & Piaget, 1958; Tanner, J. M., 1971).

During the development of the concept of a middle school, arguments were made that it should *not* include the ninth grade nor the fifth grade (Brod, 1966; Treacy, 1968). Several types of middle-school-grade organizations have emerged over the past 20 years such as 5-6-7-8, 6-7-8, and 7-8.

Throughout the 1960s and 1970s the whole issue of the middle school's rationale, purposes, organization, and differences from the junior high school were widely debated (Alexander, 1964, 1978; Batezel, 1968; Brod, 1966; Brooks, 1978; Compton, 1968; Eichhorn, 1980; Malinka, 1977; Treacy, 1968). Perhaps as many as half of the middle schools exist in name only. They are the product of shifting school enrollments, building utilization, integration pressures, or economic factors rather than a unified educational rationale. From the beginning, advocates for middle schools have stressed diversity, individuality, and uniqueness as part of the middle school movement with the expectation that all middle schools would not be alike even in philosophy (Gatewood, Dilg, & Charles, 1975; George, 1977; Morrison, 1978; Toepfer, 1977; Van Til, Vars, & Lounsbury, 1967).

McConnell's summary in 1981 of the educational literature for the

period from 1960 to 1980 reveals "some commonly agreed upon characteristics possessed by 'real middle schools'" (McConnell, 1981). She
found that the desired middle school was one that has the following:

1. A program that has been specifically designed to meet the physical,
   intellectual, social, and emotional needs of the pre- and early adolescent and to cope with the problems of pre- and early adolescence.
2. A choice of exploratory programs that should give students opportunities to develop interests in aesthetic, leisure, career, and other aspects of life, including learning more about themselves.
3. An atmosphere of basic respect for the individual that can make a
   reality of individualized instruction.
4. An environment in which the student and not the program is most
   important and where the opportunity to succeed is ensured for all
   students. Development and enhancement of self-concept is recognized as an important educational goal. Self-esteem appears to have
   a stronger relationship to school achievement than either ability or
   motivation.
5. A positive and active learning environment. An active learning environment should be promoted because this is an important means
   of relating learner characteristics, such as variable attention spans,
   physical restlessness, and concrete cognitive capabilities, to subject
   matter.
6. A flexibility in facilities and scheduling that allows for a variety of
   grouping patterns and activities.
7. A setting in which every student is well known by at least one staff
   member. A teacher-counselor in a home base or advisory group setting may be that staff member. The teacher-counselor role is necessary in order to cope with the emotional and psychological crises
   that occur with this age group. Students also have a strong need to
   know and relate to an adult other than a parent.
8. A program that specifically helps pre- and early adolescents to grow
   in self-understanding and the understanding of others.
9. A choice of multiple opportunities to develop social- and human-
   relations skills in activities appropriate for the age group. Learning
   to work well in a peer group is a developmental task for pre- and
   early adolescents.
10. A concern with affective, as well as cognitive and psychomotor, de-
    velopment. The importance of affective factors as motivators—friend-
    ship, good grades, positive feedback—is acknowledged. Opportuni-
    ties for values clarification and development should be a part of the
    school program.

11. A concern with creativity and divergent thinking as well as convergent thinking. There should be many opportunities for expression of creative talents through musical and dramatic programs, student newspapers, art, and other means of expression. Students should be able to do much of the planning and carrying out of such activities on their own.

12. A way to facilitate a smooth educational transition between elementary and high school while allowing for the physical and emotional changes taking place during this stage of development. It should provide a way to mediate between the onset of adolescence and the pressures of culture—a way to continue general education applied in a psychosocial environment that is functional at this stage of socialization.

13. An educational climate that emphasizes learning how to learn. Developing abilities to solve problems, determine values, and be receptive to new facts should be a part of the educational process. The emphasis should be on inquiry rather than memorization.

14. A physical education program designed to develop conditioning and coordination. A strong intramural program should replace the traditional highly competitive athletic program.

15. A health program geared to promoting positive physical and mental health and to providing sex education appropriate for this age. Since students at this age are self-conscious in terms of rapid or slow development of secondary sex characteristics, health units should include self-image, physical development, and sex-role identification.

16. A guide for the development of mental processes, attitudes, and values needed for constructive citizenship. Students should have opportunities to be of service to others.

17. A staff of teachers who recognize and understand the students' needs, interests, backgrounds, motivations, and goals as well as fears, stresses, and frustrations and who are competent to deal with them. Since the students' attitudes toward school and schoolwork are so affected by their relationships with teachers, skillful teachers are the main ingredient in a successful middle school.

18. A variety of instructional methods appropriate for this age group. These would include individualized instruction, variable group sizes, independent study programs, and computer-assisted instruction.

19. An emphasis of diagnostic teaching. Teachers need to become diagnosticians of learning needs and resource persons who guide instruction. They also need to be able to assess the effectiveness of learning experiences in the achievement of special purposes for students.

20. A reassessment of subject matter areas with a view to a more effective

synthesis of content and the development of interdisciplinary approaches. Teams of teachers from a variety of academic pursuits should provide opportunities for students to see how areas of knowledge fit together. Interdisciplinary learning is often cited as an appropriate way to make subject matter relevant to the interests and concerns of students.

21. A school principal with effective leadership. More than anyone else, the principal determines the atmosphere, direction, and effectiveness of a school. The principal should view herself or himself as an educational leader who maintains close touch with the school program and curriculum and who involves the staff in the decision-making process.

22. An evaluation of student progress carried out in a manner that is not counterproductive to major middle school goals nor destructive to student self-esteem insofar as possible. The marking and reporting system should focus on individual growth and include some self-evaluation features. Growth is measurable; evaluation should reflect student personal growth. Student conferences as well as parent conferences should be part of the evaluation process.

23. Participation by parents and other community resource people in order to broaden the context for education. A planned program of community relations should not only involve parents and other community leaders in school programs and activities, it also should involve parents and community leaders in the decision-making process.

THE MIDDLE SCHOOL IN THE 1980s

Toward the close of the 1970s, a national concern about the fate of middle schools emerged. Research on middle schools and junior high schools revealed they were more alike than different and that there were few data to support claims of either middle school advocates or critics. Kohut found "no statistical difference between middle school and junior high school teachers in terms of understanding the philosophical purposes, goals, and actual practices of the middle school" (Kohut, 1980).

The organizers of the middle school movement envisaged this school as having its own identity and curriculum serving the biological, behavioral, and social needs of the early adolescent. The implicit assumption was that the junior high school had failed to meet the special developmental needs of children 10–14 years of age. Now the question being raised is, Why does the middle school seem to be no more effective than the junior high school? (Barnett, Handel, & Weser, 1968).

Throughout the 1970s there was a plethora of circumstances internal and external to the middle school movement that constrained its development into a viable institution. My analysis of these conditions shows (1) traditional notions of schooling; (2) integration problems; (3) a shortage of qualified teachers; (4) lack of appropriate textbooks, standardized tests, local and state curriculum guidelines; (5) vagueness of educational perspective and lack of consensus on goals; (6) failure to establish connections with both the elementary and secondary school programs; (7) weak parental and public support; (8) back-to-basics movement; (9) lack of administrative insight including that of school boards; (10) limited economic support extending to buildings and facilities; (11) pedagogical difficulties; (12) unrecognized changes in the home and culture influencing the socialization of children; (13) discipline-based school subjects isolated from one another and without interconnections; and (14) lack of academic and pedagogical leadership from colleges and universities. Hargreaves (1986) found that many of these same conditions and constraints were diminishing the effectiveness of middle schools in England.

A reexamination of the middle school began in the 1980s. A yearbook, focused on the early adolescents and their education, was prepared by the National Society for the Study of Education (M. Johnson, 1980). The theme of the book is a recognition that it is the conjunction of rapid biological, social, cognitive and emotional changes that lends special significance to pre- and early adolescence. The specialists who contributed to the yearbook agreed uniformly that intervention programs are essential for the optimal development of the early adolescent. They did not specify a school structure or a curriculum suitable for achieving the perceived urgency for interventions.

Recommendations for the improvement of middle school education in the early 1980s were initiated by professional societies (National Middle School Association, 1982; Reinhartz & Beach, 1983) and middle school specialists (Alexander & George, 1981; George, 1983). These reports served to strengthen belief in a middle school that would allow recognition of the nature and needs of the early adolescent and provide supportive educational experiences.

A comprehensive review of middle school education for the period 1964–1984 was sponsored by the National Middle School Association (Lounsbury, 1984). The committee found that although there has been universal support for middle schools, there has been little success in generating curricula based on the developmental needs of the early adolescent. The desired cross-disciplinary, integrated curriculum with a common core for all students, though widely advocated, has not yet emerged.

A national comparison of middle school and junior high school programs and practices was reported in 1983 (McEwin & Clay, 1983). The random sample included 320 middle schools and an equal number of junior high schools. Among the findings from the responding middle schools were these:

1. Eighty-seven percent of middle schools included grades 6, 7, and 8, and 13% included grades 5–8.
2. Seventy-four percent of these schools were housed in buildings designed as an elementary, junior high, or senior high school.
3. Sixty-one percent had no teachers trained for the middle school level. The largest number of teachers were certified for the elementary school.
4. Science, social studies, mathematics, and language arts were required subjects in 98% of the schools. Courses elected by students were mostly in instrumental music and vocational studies.
5. Eighty-three percent of the schools were departmentalized in a way similar to the high school.
6. Fifty-four percent of the schools used ability grouping.
7. Eighty percent of the schools had uniform periods for all subjects.
8. Interscholastic sports were a part of the student activity program in the majority of schools. Intermural sports programs were available in 60% of the schools.
9. Sixty-seven percent of the middle schools lacked an advisor-advisee guidance program.
10. Forty-eight percent of the principals had fewer than 6 years of experience.

When middle school principals were queried about their administrative problems, 80% of the problems were seen as

Resistance of teachers to change
Teachers not oriented to a middle school philosophy
Pressure for an articulation between middle schools and high schools
Lack of finances and insufficient materials to implement programs
Grouping and scheduling students
Inadequate physical plant
Pressures for more interscholastic activities—sports, bands, debate, and so on
Insufficient planning time for new programs
Developing a flexible schedule

On the whole, McEwin and Clay (1983) found that the conditions, practices, and problems of the middle school were seen as not much different from those of the junior high school.

Throughout the literature on middle school education in the early 1980s, one finds the statement that middle schools exist "to meet the needs of the developing adolescent." Almost never is there a description of these needs that is based on research findings and that could give meaning to the "needs" statement. A volume prepared by the National Academy of Sciences (NAS) Panel to Review the Status of Basic Research on School-Age Children identified needed areas of research on the cognitive, social, and emotional development of children 6 to 12 years of age (Collins, 1984). The panel confirmed observations made by teachers throughout this century that there are distinctive changes that characterize the development of adolescents. The critical importance of an intervention school program is highlighted by a panel statement:

> Middle childhood behavior and performance have repeatedly been found to predict adolescent and adult status, including social and personal disfunction, more reliably than do early childhood indicators, and this predictiveness increases over the years 6 to 12. (p. 409)

An American Academy of Arts and Sciences report, published in 1971, reviewed the need for more research on the early adolescent (Graubard, 1971). The report began with the statement "We know less about early adolescence than we ought to." A plea was made for a more systematic study of early adolescence, especially "of the condition of young people in an industrial society."

In 1978 a report prepared for the National Science Foundation (NSF) on the early adolescent called attention to the need to identify a coherent theory of early adolescent development that will serve to focus on and interpret the results of research (Hurd, 1978). The panel recognized that curriculum and instructional practices in middle schools are not likely to improve without a more thorough and comprehensive base of research on the developmental characteristics of early adolescents.

MIDDLE GRADES SCIENCE

The National Association of Secondary School Principals' Council on Middle Level Education proposed a middle school curriculum that fostered the adaptive skills of students (National Association of Secondary School Principals, 1985). These skills were described as knowing how to learn, how to adjust to change, and how to explore issues that have a base in values, ethics, morals, and the law. The council recommended a curriculum that "informs students of the forces shaping human history" and "the efforts human-kind has made to influence those forces and bring about change." Instruction should be designed to engage students in "productive thinking, systematic reasoning and the evaluation of information" and "to connect the materials and skills learned in one class to those presented in another."

Wiles and Bondi view the 1980s as a time of reviewing the middle school concept—its purposes, goals, and philosophy (Wiles & Bondi, 1986a). They note the middle school should not be regarded as a modified junior high school (Wiles & Bondi, 1986b). They propose "a well-balanced program focused on personal development, emphasizing skills for continued learning, and utilizing knowledge to foster social competence." They suggest the possibility of a curriculum based on human beings as a central theme and dealt with in the context of different school subjects such as language arts, social studies, science, and mathematics.

Dozens of research studies on the middle school and on the teaching of students at this level were reviewed by Johnson and Markle in 1986 (Johnson & Markle, 1986). They concluded that "there has not been enough research to indicate clear-cut trends" or a "framework of consensus" on policy and issues concerning the middle school. A follow-up study on needed research involved 400 randomly selected administrators and teachers, all members of the National Middle School Association. The most frequent request was for research on the "physiological and psychological developmental characteristics affecting school performance which are unique to students at this level." Ranking second was the importance of identifying the characteristics of successful middle school teachers.

Based on a distillation of recent writings on middle school education and extensive public hearings, a California Task Force had the following recommendations for improving the education of the early adolescent:

1. A core curriculum, including a science-health component, should be required of all students. It was noted that this core must be different in concept from core programs of the past.
2. The subject matter of the core program should be linked directly to young adolescents and how they fit into the world about them and should be appropriate "to the developmental characteristics of young adolescents."
3. Learning to learn, and thinking and communication processes, should be dealt with directly and integrated with the knowledge components of the curriculum. This approach is in contrast to the "segmented, compartmentalized, and fragmented" curriculum found in most middle schools. (Report of the Superintendents' Middle Grades Task Force, 1987)

The report emphasized the importance of instructional practices that systematically enable students to do for themselves whatever each subject requires—in other words, to become independent learners. The application of knowledge is considered an essential attribute of "active learning." The California Task Force views the middle school instructional organization as a transition between the elementary grades and high school—less self-contained than in the elementary grades and less departmentalized than in high schools.

During the 1980s the proponents of the middle school concept reaffirmed their belief that the best educational setting for early adolescence is a special kind of school. Little new has been added to the arguments supporting middle schools, either in philosophy or practice. There is a recognition that the social conditions under which young people live and must respond to today are different from those of the 1970s and 1980s. The research essential for identifying the conditions and constraints on early adolescent development is currently limited and unfocused. Teachers for the middle school continue to be poorly prepared both academically and pedagogically for the tasks expected of them. The rigidities within education and the disassociation of social, behavioral, and developmental research from any direct relation to schooling leave the education of young people at about the status it has had for the last 100 years.

4

Rethinking Education in the Middle Grades

A wave of criticism extending to all precollege education began in the late 1970s. The middle school at that time was in the process of establishing its identity and clarifying its educational philosophy. Critics of middle schools pointed out that there was little research to support their claims of worthiness as a distinctive institution. Two decades of educational speculation and surveys of middle school practices provided no clear-cut answers to questions raised by critics. There were parents and educators, however, who were convinced that some middle schools were more effective in achieving desired educational results with early adolescents than were other intermediate schools. Studies of those schools have mostly been limited to directives, mechanisms, or organizational factors that are readily observable rather than the quality of education for young teenagers being evaluated.

The purpose of this chapter is to review conditions and issues that are influencing the reform of middle school education.

A summary of observations derived from case studies of effective middle schools reveals more commonalities than differences. Typically, an effective middle school is identified as having some combination of at least five to seven of the following factors:

- Principal exerts strong positive leadership and selects staff members with a middle school orientation.
- Staff has internalized a philosophical context for school improvement and works with a sense of mission.
- Staff morale is high, teachers cooperate with one another and with the school's administration; there is collaborative action in decision making.
- Schools have a staff development program that teachers accept.
- School programs for improvement are projected for a period of several years.
- School has a reputation as a "good" or "effective" place for emerging adolescents.

- Schools are not too large, 300–400 students or if larger are organized as a school within a school.
- Time is made available for teachers to plan curricula, to provide individual counseling, and to interact with students in out-of-class activities.
- Funding is available for equipment, services, and a staff instructional-materials center.
- Parents are cooperative, participate in school affairs, and frequently volunteer their services.
- School is recognized in the community and has broad community support for school activities.
- Instructional materials are focused on goals, evaluated frequently, and modified to make improvements.
- Efforts are made to reduce departmentalization in the school curriculum and increase interdisciplinary work.
- Positive efforts are made by teachers to meet the common needs of early adolescents as well as those of individuals.
- A teacher advisor is provided for each student in addition to there being guidance counselors.
- Homogeneous grouping for students allows them to experience a common core of knowledge and improve socialization.
- Curriculum offerings are diversified to meet the interests of different students.
- School has a positive learning climate.
- High expectations exist for all students, with a focus on independent learning and higher order thinking skills.
- School has a low rate of student absenteeism, few dropouts, and a minimal number of suspensions.
- An extensive program of out-of-class activities for students is provided: clubs, social events, debating and intramural teams, programs for participation in school and community affairs, physical activities, and opportunities for interaction with adults. (Barnett, Handel, & Weser, 1968; DeVita, Pumerantz, & Wilkiow, 1970; Dorman, 1987; Frymier et al., 1984; George & Oldoker, 1985; Levine, Levine, & Eubanks, 1984; Morrison, 1978; Tye, 1985; University of Southern California, 1979)

Middle school research does not provide precise evidence of what it is that children learn in middle schools that advances their biological, social, and behavioral development as emerging adolescents. The school climate and conditions deemed necessary to make a middle school curriculum function properly are described, and there is a fair degree of consensus about what these are. Curriculum patterns essential to accomplishing the goals of middle schools either do not exist or are not reported. Joan Lipsitz in her book *Successful Schools for Young Adolescents* (1984) comments:

> Translating philosophy into curriculum is the most difficult feat for schools to accomplish. The translation to climate and organizational structure appears to be much easier for these schools than the translation of purpose into curriculum. (p. 188)

Tye in his study of over 350 middle/junior high school classes found that rarely do the subjects taught reflect the developmental needs of students or our unique society (1985, p. 3). He notes that although philosophical differences are recognized between middle and junior high school these differences are not found in practice.

In a report to the Alfred P. Sloan Foundation, the investigators found that science teachers are not actively seeking a new curriculum, although they recognize that what they are now teaching is disliked by the majority of students (University of Southern California, 1979). Furthermore, teachers were not supportive of the idea of integrating science with other subjects or relating science to societal issues, to real life, or to the real world. The researchers concluded that teachers are not interested in curriculum changes unless it makes the task of teaching easier. To change this attitude will require a much more powerful appeal to teachers than the promise of educational effectiveness. Policy studies are needed to establish the basic themes of what is required to improve the education of the early adolescent in terms of current social and cultural changes (National Research Council, 1985).

SCIENCE IN THE MIDDLE/JUNIOR HIGH SCHOOL

The first major effort to improve the teaching of science in the junior high school was in 1915 with the introduction of general science. The subject matter of these courses was a sampling of topics in biology, physics, chemistry, and geology. Courses were rich in examples of how science was influencing industrial development in the United States. The radio, automobile, and airplane, electrical appliances, animal breeding, new farming methods, and health and sanitation practices were featured as well as laboratory demonstrations and experiments. The primary reason for introducing general science into the curriculum was to stimulate student interest in taking more science courses in the secondary schools where enrollments had been decreasing since the turn of this century. In the years following its introduction, general science became the most popular science course in the intermediate school curriculum; however, it did not stimulate students to take more science in high school.

A national effort to reform the teaching of science in schools was initiated by the National Science Foundation (NSF) in the late 1950s. Under the rubric of "course content improvement," NSF enlisted the interest of scientists in various disciplines to upgrade school science courses. The reform began with high school science offerings followed by new programs for the elementary school. Late in the 1960s, attention was directed toward improving junior high school science. The rationale, goals, and subject matter of these new courses were described by Hurd (1970) in his book *New Curriculum Perspectives for Junior High School Science*.

Twenty-two junior high school science programs were initiated. General science was largely replaced by courses in life science, earth science, and physical science to better represent the academic context of the disciplines and their modes of inquiry. Standards were identified as the principles and generalizations of a science discipline.

THE PUBLIC SPEAKS OUT ON MIDDLE SCHOOL EDUCATION

In March 1970 the NSF recognized the need to transform science education at every school level. The NSF's new position was to shift science education from a focus on academic disciplines to one stressing "interdisciplinary approaches centered upon problems faced by informed citizens" (NSF, 1970, p. iii).

At the same time a series of middle school curriculum studies were initiated to consider more explicitly the developmental needs of the early adolescent. Although this has been a goal of early adolescence education for the past 100 years, action has been more rhetorical than a road map for a curriculum transformation in the middle grades. An exception was a program developed by the Biological Sciences Curriculum Study (BSCS), which had a "human biology" focus, recognizing the early adolescent as the major criterion for guiding a curriculum transformation.

The 1980s to the present time represent a period in which the general public, agencies of the federal government, and educational foundations have sought to clarify the basic themes and goal of middle grades education. The wealth of social and cultural changes now taking place demand a fresh and more positive approach to the education of early adolescents, one that serves the choices they must make for a productive and healthy life.

In 1981, a study by Hurd, Robinson, McConnell, and Ross (1981) identified the following current trends, conditions, and voids in the education of early adolescents:

- In 1980, the ratio of junior high schools to middle schools in the United States was 3 to 2. Although the number of middle schools increased by 50% during the previous 2 years, approximately 75% of the students were enrolled in junior high schools.
- Early adolescents attended a variety of institutional arrangements including grades 7–9, 7–8, 6–8, 5–8, 5–9, K–8, 7–12, and K–12.
- The science curriculum had shifted from a general science context to a program of separated courses in life, physical, and earth science. The number of schools with each arrangement was about equal, but the largest number of students were enrolled in the traditional general science course.
- Those middle school students who were male, White, and had at least one parent with a post-high-school education as well as all students who lived in advantaged urban areas or in the suburbs of large cities scored above national norms in science on National Assessment of Educational Progress (NAEP) tests.
- Females, Blacks, and students whose parents did not graduate from high school or who lived in the southeastern region of the United States or in big cities performed below national norms on the NAEP tests. The results of the NAEP tests indicated that by age 13, the social, economic, ethnic, and cultural environments of students influence science achievement far more than schooling does.
- The typical science teacher in the middle or junior high school was not trained for this level of education. Based on their experience in schools they wished they had had (a) a stronger background in science, (b) more preservice experience, (c) courses in science teaching methods, and (d) courses in understanding early adolescents and the management of their behavior.
- More than 60% of the junior high schools used homogeneous grouping for classes.
- Trained counselors were located in most middle schools but in only 4% of the schools was there one counselor for each group of 200 pupils (considered to be the ideal ratio).
- Only 20% of science teachers felt they had adequate facilities for teaching science.
- The science curriculum in 80% of the schools was a single textbook, and in 10% of the schools teachers prepared their own materials.
- About half of middle and junior high school teachers had attended in-

service programs but felt they were not very helpful in solving pedagogical problems.

- "Good" science teachers found NSF summer institutes worthwhile but
  only a third of the teachers had attended a science institute.
- Middle school teachers viewed instructional management, student discipline, the poor reading skills of pupils, and lack of student motivation as their most serious problems.
- Students in middle schools generally were lukewarm about taking science courses; they felt that there was too much to memorize. But at
  the same time they found classes interesting and believed science to
  be important.
- Somewhat more than half of the science teachers, as well as parents,
  objected to the teaching of controversial issues such as science-technol-
  ogy-societal problems, biological evolution, and human sexuality.
- Although the rationale and goals of middle school education call for a
  science curriculum suited to the developmental aspects of the early
  adolescent, no such curriculum was found in the schools. Also absent
  from the science curriculum, although widely recommended, were
  such attributes as (a) the social significance of science and technology,
  (b) considerations of values and ethics in science and technology, (c)
  the utilization of science knowledge, (d) logical reasoning and decision
  making, (e) a future perspective in terms of changes and progress in
  science and technology, and (f) career awareness in the sciences and
  engineering.

These findings have been substantiated by other investigators using
a similar database such as the report to the Sloan Foundation on science
education for the early adolescent (University of Southern California,
1979).

THE CONDITION AND STATUS OF MIDDLE/JUNIOR HIGH SCHOOL
SCIENCE EDUCATION IN THE 1980s

In 1981, 21 science education specialists reviewed promising practices in
science education in middle schools (Ochs, 1981). Although no consensus
statement was developed, the writers agreed that the science curriculum
should be structured more in terms of student interests, social concerns,
the human agenda, and human ecology. The present middle school science curriculum was viewed as simply a "writing down" of high school
courses.

A comparison of the results of three national assessments of science was reported in 1983 (Hueftle, Rakow, & Welch, 1983). In general, 13-year-old students did not show a decline in their knowledge of science compared with previous assessments, and in biology they were doing somewhat better. The test results show that students are best in their knowledge of plant and animal systems, cell theory, and ecology. They were poorly informed in the areas of energy transformation and evolution. Boys were only slightly better than girls in terms of biological information. Roughly half of the 13-year-olds had a positive attitude toward science; a third found science to be fun, and three fourths thought it boring. Nearly two thirds of the students had a positive feeling about their teachers.

By the age of 13, 50% of the students have had a course in life science; 34.2% had the course in the seventh grade and 19.8% in the eighth grade. In terms of the total number of students enrolled at a grade level, 42% are taking life science in Grade 7 and 12% in Grade 8. These percentages vary in different sections of the country. For example, 53% of seventh graders in the West take life science, whereas only 31% do so in the central states; the ratio is the reverse for grade 8.

A more detailed study of ethnic differences in middle schools was made by the Educational Testing Service for the Ford Foundation (Lockheed, Thorpe, Brooks-Gunn, Casserly, & Meloon, 1985). The authors found (a) little recent research has been conducted that directly addresses either gender differences within ethnicity or gender-ethnicity interactions, or that examines the factors that are related to the achievement of minority girls per se, in grades 4–8; (b) virtually no empirical studies on the determinants of middle school student participation in mathematics, science, or computer-related learning activities have been conducted; and (c) the primary focus of most empirical studies of factors related to participation and performance has been on the affective rather than on policy-oriented factors.

In 1980 the NSF funded a study of middle school science education programs (Weiss, 1980). Among the findings of this report were the following:

- The goals of science curricula currently found in middle schools are focused almost solely on academic preparation, largely ignoring goals related to the use of science in everyday life, societal decision making, and career choice. Middle school science should address the needs of all students in the context of a democratic society that is highly technological.
- The present science curriculum in middle schools was found to be

a "turn off" for two out of three students, from a further study of science.

- An interdisciplinary approach to the curriculum is recommended, using problems and issues of interest to early adolescents as the vehicle for learning fundamental principles and engaging students in how to do science.
- Curriculum development should be backed with research on the needs of early adolescents. Additional research is also needed on pedagogy and evaluation that are in harmony with the rationale and goals of middle school science.
- Teachers were most unsure about how to teach higher order thinking skills such as the processing of information, decision making, making informed judgments, and communicating information.
- Teachers were uncertain about how to incorporate ideas about the interrelationships of science, technology, and society. A substantial number of the respondents identified the issue as one of using computers rather than the interrelationship of science and technology.
- The survey revealed that the science curricula in schools are moving from local control to the state level. This is accomplished through state-mandated curricula or state-adopted textbooks.
- Although there was an opportunity to do so in the survey document, fewer than a half-dozen respondents made specific reference to the early adolescent as a person and a central figure in curriculum reform.

Blosser (1983) reviewed studies on science teaching in middle schools historically and currently. She considered the learning and developmental studies associated with Piaget, Bruner, and Gagné to be particularly relevant for establishing realistic goals and curricula for middle school students.

Another part of her study considers problems of pre- and in-service education of middle school science teachers and the lack of special training and skills for effectively teaching early adolescents. Blosser notes that research data on the teaching and student learning of science in middle schools is unorganized and insufficient for planning the best possible curriculum. She also concludes that a more comprehensive conceptual framework and a clarification of goals for science education in the middle schools is needed.

The Education Commission of the States in 1986 conducted a 50-state survey of middle/junior high school science initiatives and issues (Armstrong, Mayer, & Wilkins, 1986). Information was collected on curriculum frameworks, graduation requirements, time requirements, special schools or programs, student recognition programs, textbook adoption policies, student assessment, funding, serving underrepresented groups, and suggested roles for the NSF. The major problems and issues that emerged from the study were the following:

- Respondents rated the shortage of qualified middle school science teachers as the most serious problem. The shortage also extends to the number of teachers preparing to teach in middle schools. The range in percentage of unqualified teachers by states is 30% to 80% with a national average of 50%.
- Most states have plans to finance a variety of in-service educational programs.
- The second most frequently cited problem in middle school science instruction was a shortage of laboratory facilities, equipment, and materials. Of the 18 states providing increased funding for science instruction only 3 states made a provision for additional funds for laboratory equipment.
- Respondents ranked development of a high-quality middle school science curriculum as a major priority in their states. Especially needed are instructional materials appropriate to middle grade ability and interests of students.
- Sixteen states have state-mandated science curricula, frameworks, or guides, and another 25 model science curricula available. Respondents nevertheless indicated a need for well-developed, up-to-date science curriculum aimed at students in middle schools.
- Teachers are critical of middle school science textbooks for their failure to take into account the psychological developmental states of children of middle school age. Teachers want textbooks that consider the interface between science, technology, and society. Science supervisors report that they are unable to locate "any real research" on what science should be taught at the middle school level.
- A persistent and serious issue is the lack of student motivation for the study of science. Courses are needed that stress scientific literacy and everyday applications.
- Teacher apathy is another problem in the middle school, the result of a perceived isolation and limited interaction with other teachers and professionals.
- In about half of the states, some use is made of computers in teaching science, but appropriate software is limited.

In summary, the 50-state survey revealed that middle grade teachers "want new, updated curriculum materials, inservice and ideas about labs." Teachers state they need help in determining what science subject matter is appropriate for middle grade students and in clarifying the answers to the questions "What is the mission of the middle school as it relates to science instruction? What are the needs of and characteristics of early learners, skills to be developed and scope of the curriculum?"

In making a secondary analysis of 50-state survey data, I found the following to be the case:

- In more than half of the states the final choice of science textbooks is locally controlled, though the state may provide standards. The textbook adoption cycle was typically 5 years, ranging to 10 years.
- The subject matter of the middle school science curriculum should include a dimension that informs all boys and girls of career options in science, engineering, and technical fields.
- The introduction and implementation of a new curriculum into schools are difficult processes. A first step is to create a level of awareness in the field in terms of purposes, rationale, and goals.
- To be effective in a reform of the middle school science curriculum, the goals must be made familiar to state and local school boards, school administrators, and principals, as well as teachers and parents.
- There is little to be gained in the reform of middle school science unless teachers have adequate facilities, equipment, and teaching materials.
- A persistent problem in middle schools is the shortage of qualified science teachers. The nature of the education necessary has not been fully determined. It is clear that the teacher's preparation should be consistent with the nature of the curriculum and the educational goals they are expected to implement.

The National Middle School Association (1983) has formulated guidelines for the professional certification and preparation of middle school teachers. The report notes that middle school teachers need preparation in at least two academic fields. The association found that there were few opportunities for middle school teachers to obtain graduate preparation. In 1982 only 13% of teacher-preparation institutions reported having middle-level master's degree programs and equally rare were programs for in-service or renewal education. The report emphasized that the preparation of middle school teachers should not be like that of elementary or secondary school teachers.

The National Science Teachers Association (NSTA) has developed standards for the preparation of science teachers for the middle/junior high school levels (Standing Committee on Teacher Education, 1986). The standards committee noted the absence of science majors in colleges and universities and of science methods courses specially planned for the preparation of middle school science teachers. The implementation of standards at the present time would require colleges and universities to establish a broad-field major in the sciences and in schools of education to develop new courses on middle school pedagogy.

NSTA has established a journal and formulated guidelines for the improvement of middle school science education. The NSTA committee took the position that middle-level science courses should fulfill the needs of the early adolescent rather than focus on preparation for a higher grade level. The science curriculum should "reflect society's goals for scientific and technological literacy and emphasize the role of science for personal, social, and career use, as well as prepare students academically."

In 1986, the Carnegie Council on Adolescent Development began its 10-year study of today's adolescents and their education. A national task force was appointed to consider various dimensions of the 100-year-old problem. Its report, titled *Turning Points: Preparing American Youth for the 21st Century* (1989), is regarded as the most comprehensive study available on adolescents and the need for a transformation of middle grades curricula.

The NSF is currently supporting various programs related to middle schools including materials development (NSF, 1987), informal science programs (NSF, 1986), and teacher education (NSF, 1986). A companion volume to *Turning Points* was published by the Carnegie Council in 1995 that deals specifically with the healthy development of America's 10- to 15-year-olds (Carnegie Council on Adolescent Development, 1995; see also Hechinger, 1992).

A center was established in Washington, DC, to study what we know about adolescents and how that knowledge can be put to use to meet the needs of early adolescents in today's world (Takanishi, 1993, pp. 1–7). In the past, studies of adolescent development have mostly been limited to biological characteristics. Currently the view of adolescence is that it is a combination of interactions between biological drives and social factors interacting in ways that determine human behavior. Both these dimensions are seen as basic to curriculum transformations that enable adolescents to understand self and others (Feldman & Elliott, 1990).

Studies by the Carnegie Council on Adolescent Development (1989, pp. 9–10) recommend the following factors they deemed essential for transforming the middle grades:

• Create small communities for learning in which every student is known well by at least one adult.

- Teach a core academic program that results in students who are literate, including in the sciences, who know how to think critically, lead a healthy life, behave ethically, and assume the responsibilities of citizenship in a pluralistic society.
- Ensure success for all students through the elimination of tracking and the promotion of cooperative learning.
- Empower teachers and administrators to make decisions about experiences for middle grade students through creative control by teachers over the instructional program, one tailored to enhance the intellectual and emotional development of all youth.
- Staff middle grade schools with teachers who are expert at teaching young adolescents and have been specially prepared for assignment to the middle grades.
- Improve academic performance through fostering the health and fitness of young adolescents, by providing a health coordinator in every middle grade school.
- Engage families in the education of young adolescents by giving families meaningful roles in school governance.
- Connect schools with communities, which together share responsibility for each middle grade student's success.

The Carnegie Council recognized a need to establish a national task force on the entire problem of middle school education for the new millennium, marked by social, cultural, scientific, personal, and economic changes. There is supportive research and educational experience for many, but not all, of the factors that are essential for an effective middle school. One problem is the lack of a permanent national task force or a forum focused on the standards that are essential for the preparation of developing adolescents, in order to provide them with an understanding of themselves and of the dimensions of a productive life in the 21st century. The problem is acute in that the choices students must make are for a period in history that none of us have experienced. Progress along these lines has been summarized by Feldman and Elliott (1990).

It is estimated that one in four early adolescents is in serious trouble with school, drugs, or crime. How these problems can be dealt with by schools and parents is summarized in a public agenda monograph (Public Agenda, 1997). The report recommends and outlines ways of dealing with the 7 million young people who are at risk, recognizing that there is no one procedure that fits all school situations. What is common is that evolutionary changes in our culture and society pose adaptation issues for early adolescents today as in no other period in the nation's history.

A review of the studies reported in this chapter leads to the conclusion that from any aspect—student, teacher, curriculum, or administrative policy—the entire issue of the best science education for the early adolescent remains. There is no end of statements and committee reports identifying the problem, but as yet no mechanism or concerted leadership has developed to focus and sustain the essential actions for reform and a road map for transforming the science curriculum.

5

Emerging Goals for the Teaching of Science

In the first four chapters of this book I consider characteristics of early adolescence and the restructuring of the middle schools. In devising a modern science curriculum, the first step is to identify the personal and social needs of the age groups for which the curriculum is intended.

A second step is to identify national goals for the teaching of science at precollege education levels. The United States is one of only five countries in the world that do not have a national curriculum. The development of a road map for modernizing science education goals depends upon flushing out from some 400 science reform reports, published since 1970, their vision of what science teaching changes should be about. This chapter identifies my synthesis of those reports, their visions and basic themes for transforming education in the sciences.

There is broad agreement that the traditional goals and subject matter of middle school science curricula are obsolete. "In recent years, the contexts in which science and technology are performed in the United States have undergone fundamental changes—changes that will continue into the future" (Committee on Science, Engineering, and Public Policy, 1993, p. 1). So far, science curriculum reform efforts have been simply a matter of updating and making existing courses more rigorous rather than the invention of new curricula.

Science/technology as a whole has become an integral part of our economic, social, personal, and political lives. Paradigm shifts in the culture and practice of today's science "call for more creative forms of collaboration between scientists and society and for a broader range of disciplines and competencies to take part in the process" (Jasanoff et al., 1997). The path from research to human benefit has been shortened and made more relevant. The meaning of today's science extends beyond the facts, theories, and laws characteristic of the discipline-bound science curricula that are now typical of science textbooks. Currently the traditional disciplines of science—biology, chemistry, earth science, and physics—have been broken into numerous research *fields*. Biology, for example, has been fractionated into more than 400 named research fields, and as knowledge in each field increases they are again fractionated to be more comprehensible for researchers, but as it turns out, they are less so in the context of a citizen's education in science.

There was a time when advances in technology were generated by the sciences. Today it is technology that determines the limits of a science. Witness the Hubble space telescope, which has extended our observations of the universe, and the scanning tunneling microscope, which makes it possible to observe chemical bonding in a single cell. The relationship of science/technology is now viewed as two sides of a single coin.

Most research in the sciences today is strategic, targeted, or problem oriented rather than hypothesis or theory driven. Studies on the control of the AIDS pandemic are an example of problem-oriented research. Increasingly, research is done by a team assisted by computers that keep track of observations and sometimes help to organize data. A major advantage of team research is that it increases the fertility of hypotheses in resolving problems. Research teams usually consist of six to eight scientists representing different fields.

Science research is becoming more cross- or transdisciplinary, relating the natural and social sciences for the planning of human resources such as agriculture, health, education, and the environment. In the past the social benefits of science/technology have been largely fortuitous. Currently the leading edge of scientific research is located in the biological sciences as they continue to absorb the physical sciences into fields such as biochemistry, biophysics, biogeochemistry, biomedicine, and biotechnology.

Traditionally the focus of science teaching has been on presumed inquiry procedures used by scientists. Students are expected to learn and practice these processes and "think like a scientist." However, there is no standard method for the practice of science. Today research in the sciences is viewed more as a craft or an art, more as problem solving.

The center for scientific research has moved from the university to industry. It is estimated that two thirds of science researchers today are employed in industry, and the percentage is increasing. In industry the practice of science is expected to produce useable knowledge. Science/technology curricula are viewed as sterile unless they can be applied in human and social contexts (Lewenstein, 1992).

Overall, since the 1970s a trend in science has been its socialization and humanization. Values, ethics, and law have become a matter of research in the sciences: Witness the debate on DNA fingerprinting of all humans worldwide and the cloning of animals by using human genes.

LEARNING TO LEARN

Over the past 25 years "learning to learn" has become the only goal common to all countries seeking to transform science education. In the United States, building a lifelong learning behavior is viewed as an essential goal for a productive life in a knowledge-intensive era (National Education Goals Panel, 1991). The learning-to-learn issue has raised questions about what, of all that is known in the sciences, every student should know. What does it mean to know science? Knowing implies the ability to manage and put knowledge to work in resolving personal, social, and economic needs and issues (Carnegie Commission, 1994).

Currently, science curricula stress inquiry or how science information is achieved by researchers as a major goal of instruction in science—a static view of knowledge. By contrast, learning to learn as a goal seeks to engage students in an active concept of science information, one that has meaning in human affairs and is focused on the optimal utilization of knowledge. The ability to utilize knowledge is the chief adaptive factor in the evolution of the human species.

Quite independently, at the onset of the learning-to-learn concept as a science education goal, there has been the development of information technology. The textbook in its present form can no longer serve the information needs for life in our revolutionary age of change. The science education reform task now becomes "a matter of connecting instruction to the new information highway" (Cohen, 1997; McKinsey and Co., 1997; President's Committee of Advisors on Science and Technology, 1997; U.S. Department of Education, 1997).

The education challenge is a matter of how to access, synthesize, codify, and interpret science information into knowledge that can be used in personal and civic contexts. Throughout the history of science education, the sciences have been disconnected from the real world of life and living. Learning to learn is an endeavor to introduce students to knowledge in a way that enables them to travel on their own throughout life as responsible citizens and productive workers. The new vision of lifelong learning includes the building of human capital that allows students to meet the requirements of career changes throughout life (Commission for a Nation of Lifelong Learners, 1997). Most occupations today are based on knowledge rather than on mechanical skills; this makes learning to learn a need throughout life.

SCIENTIFIC LITERACY

Since the 1950s, almost all of the reports on the reform of education in the sciences have used the term *scientific literacy* to indicate a purpose for teaching science. A consensus on what that term should mean for the teaching of science is just now emerging. The roots of a meaning for scientific literacy date back to 1620, when Francis Bacon wrote, "The ideal of human service is the ultimate goal of scientific effort" (Dick, 1955, p. 441). In 1859, Herbert Spencer examined the question, asking, "What knowledge is of most worth?" He agreed with Bacon that the subject matter of school science courses should have a "bearing on some part of life." He noted that the science courses at that time consisted of a collection of "dead facts" that "fail to make clear any appreciable efforts they can produce on human welfare" (Spencer, 1860, pp. 5 and 83).

In 1743, Benjamin Franklin founded the American Philosophical Society, with the primary purpose to "promote useful knowledge and improve the scientific experience, observations, and experiments which if well examined, pursued, and improved might lead to discoveries to the advantage of some or all the nation's plantations and to the benefit of mankind in general" (Franklin, 1743). James Wilkinson, a member of the Royal College of Surgeons of London, presented a lecture in 1847 titled *Science for All*, in which he noted that the ends for which scientists create knowledge and those who seek the application of knowledge are not the same. Scientists view knowledge as a private possession without regard for public service; they want to be judged by their own peers and their own intensions rather than by their findings on the business of life (Wilkinson, 1847).

For more than 350 years, research scientists, mostly located in colleges and universities, have managed to block the teaching of science in schools and colleges that relates science to human welfare, the common good, our culture, and social and economic progress. In 1958 Paul Hurd adopted the phrase "scientific literacy" to focus discussions on a future for science education that fosters a conceptual framework that does more than maintain ignorance about the contribution of science to our culture and practical applications (Hurd, 1958).

The United States House of Representatives has proposed a new image of the sciences in regard to both research and education (U.S. Congress, House Committee on Science, 1998). The term "science" in this report is used in its broadest form, and unless stated otherwise, should be "interpreted as including the physical, natural, life and social science" (p. ii). In terms of this broad view, the purpose of middle school education is to select those concepts and principles of science relevant to our daily life and adaptive needs. It is the scientist's responsibility to provide the information, suggest its usefulness, and identify the risks in its use (p. 36). Scientists are seen as brokers of knowledge (p. 36).

Scientists today have the responsibility of providing individuals, society, and corporations with the basis for making decisions. The focus of science education today is on the use of science information in decision making, not on scientific modes of inquiry. The process of inquiring in the sciences today is evolutionary; it is a never ending process (p. 39).

"The practice of science is becoming increasingly interdisciplinary, and scientific progress in one discipline is often propelled by advances in another, or often unrelated fields" (p. 17). Who would have thought that research on the inner working of the atomic nucleus would lead ultimately to magnetic resonance imaging (MRI) as a tool to diagnose illness? The interdisciplinary character of science today serves to render obsolete discipline-bound courses—biology, earth science, chemistry, and physics—that now typify school science courses.

Since 1945, basic research in the sciences has shifted from the search for theories to research that is targeted on a known problem, such as a cure for AIDS, maintaining the quality of the natural environment, or lifelong wellness. These endeavors are known as mission-oriented research, and their purpose is to neutralize the vacuum that has long existed between science and society and between science and human welfare.

The current efforts to effect reform in the teaching of science are for the most part meaningless because most attempts are designed more to "fix" traditional concepts of the culture and practice of science than to consider attributes of the changing image of science, the emerging knowledge-intensive age, the global economy, and the changing needs of students as well as the changing world of work.

Scientific literacy is a recognition of the proactive relationships between science and society, a form of enlightenment for this age of science (Hurd, 1958). Although this view of public education in the sciences has been repeatedly sought over the past 350 years, it is only now that the scientific community is taking an active role in recognizing that a general education in the sciences organized along the traditional disciplinary lines is not adequate for life in the new millennium. Members of the American Association for the Advancement of Science (AAAS) have established committees to explore new science paradigms relating science/technology and public policy as well as research in the sciences (Jasanoff et al., 1997).

New policies for the practice of science that entail human welfare and the public good set equally new goals for the teaching of sciences in schools, colleges, and universities. Those designing and implementing school and college science curricula from this perspective have a responsibility for translating the findings of science into a language that people can understand and know how to utilize in resolving personal and social problems. Intellectual skills for the rational utilization of science knowledge include those associated with solving problems, forming judgments, making decisions, evaluating short- and long-term risks, and recognizing the influence of ethics, values, and sometimes morals when it comes to using science knowledge in personal-social contexts (Hurd, 1998). This approach views students as consumers of science information.

At this time it is unclear just what the new science curricula will be like, except for the fact that they will not resemble those traditionally found in schools and universities. Probably the best example is found in medical research, where new discoveries are translated in medical schools for the education of doctors, who in turn devise a language through which to communicate the findings to patients.

LINKING SCIENCE EDUCATION WITH THE WORKPLACE

For more than 200 years, a major goal of science teaching has been to prepare students for a career in science. Today only 1.59% of university graduates seek a career in science ("Freshman Characteristics and Attitudes," 1984). Science teachers and educators have generally held a disdain for science goals related to work in general. The onset of the information age has led to a majority of students now becoming knowledge workers. Science is seen as having a responsibility for the building of human capital in a way that will enhance the economic productivity of students.

The Workforce Readiness Act passed by the U.S. House of Representatives recommends "developing or adapting curricula and instructional materials which incorporate generic workplace skills" (H.R. No. 4078, 1992). The School-to-Work Opportunities Act, signed into law by President Clinton, is focused on the need for schools to prepare students for occupational advancement, an attribute to be shared by all school subjects. The law points out that currently "the United States lacks a comprehensive and coherent system to help its youth acquire the knowledge, skills, abilities, and information about and access to the labor market necessary to make an effective transition from school to career-oriented work or to further education and training" (H.R. No. 2884, 1994). In 1992 the U.S. Department of Labor published a 425-page report identifying the major competencies, skills, and personal qualities for entering the workforce upon completing high school (SCANS, 1992).

An average of 40 years of one's lifetime is devoted to some kind of work. Courses in school science are seen as having a responsibility for helping to prepare students for this period of their life (Marshall & Tucker, 1992; Olson, 1997; Wirth, 1992). Providing students with workplace skills for a knowledge-intensive age is not the same in perspective as the traditional notions of vocational, career education, or job training. Curriculum reform for the information age seeks to produce citizens with higher order thinking skills, intellectual adaptability, and the ability to manage knowledge and make rational decisions.

The world of work today is more complex than in the past and will likely be more so in the future. It is estimated that by the year 2000, 60% of all jobs will require skills in the use of computers (Cohen, 1997; President's Committee of Advisors on Science and Technology, 1997; U.S. Department of Education, 1996). The generic work skills sought are those associated with the access, processing, and utilization of knowledge. These skills are also primary goals of education in the sciences. What is lacking is an awareness by both teachers and students that precollege education is a matter of building human capital for today's labor market. Although distinguishing features of today's workplace have been at least partly described, more data on the demands of the world of work are needed to formulate a supporting school science curriculum.

MODERNIZING SCIENCE CURRICULA: AN EMERGING VISION

A central theme for reinventing science curricula is to put science into service for individuals and for society. This concept was proposed by the Advisory Committee for Science Education of the NSF in 1970 with the recommendation "to educate scientists who will be at home in society and to educate a society that will be at home with science" (NSF, 1970). This position is a reversal of the NSF-supported discipline-bound courses of the 1950s and 1960s. Goals for research in the sciences and in technology in terms of societal needs are also perceived as a base for reinventing school science curricula.

The educational standards being sought are those that are operational in understanding oneself, the common good, human welfare, social and economic progress, and success in the workplace. The framework for these goals is found in the nature and practice of contemporary science, a knowledge-intensive age, and the development of life skills oriented toward the forseeable future.

A base for a reform of science education is embedded in the practice and culture of contemporary science/technology, which has a focus on the interaction of natural and social systems. Some examples of the core themes reflected in the new paradigms of science are those of health and wellness, stabilizing the global environment, new energy resources, the quality of life, and the world of work. New curriculum standards are focused upon the utilization of science/technology knowledge as it enhances the adaptive needs of students. The traditional fragmented discipline-bound courses are seen as meaningless for dealing with human and social affairs, with the result that forgetting becomes a major outcome of science courses. Glenn T. Seaborg, a Nobel Prize–winning chemist, notes that we are graduating high school students as foreigners in their own culture.

Linking science/technology as a knowledge-producing system with society as a knowledge-using system is the challenge now confronting education in the sciences. The socialization and humanization of research in today's sciences provide a base for modernizing school and college science curricula. Overall, the reformation of science curricula is to move students from passive learning to a more proactive role emphasizing the personal and social use of knowledge.

Science courses over the past three centuries have stressed scientific inquiry as essential for a career in a science. The new paradigm of science education emphasizes higher learning skills and intellectual processes related to problem solving and decision making. Traditionally, science curricula have focused on the past achievements of scientists. The emphasis sought in the reinvention of science curricula is more on the future, the unresolved issues currently confronting science and society, such as the control of emerging diseases, biotechnology, and human nutrition; a better understanding of the nature of our universe; new communication systems; and climate control. This approach recognizes that life is lived forward and everyone has a responsibility for helping shape the future. The future is where all students will be spending their lives. Current science curricula are viewed as antiquated and obsolete in terms of providing a lifelong education in the sciences.

THE TASK AHEAD: A NEW VISION OF SCIENCE EDUCATION

After 25 years of debate and hundreds of national reports on what education in the sciences should be about, there is yet to emerge a unifying framework for an ongoing reform of education in the sciences. We need a clear and coherent vision of the place of science/technology in human affairs. A distillation of the literature on the transformation of science education finds a general agreement that the existing discipline-bound curricula are for the most part archaic. They fail to recognize the current practices and culture of science/technology itself. They also neglect to consider the application of science/technology in human affairs, such as the civic, work, personal, social, and economic aspects of life.

So far most actions for the reform of science education have been simply a matter of degree; they are not a reinvention of curricula containing goals that are consistent with changes taking place in the practice of today's science, a global economy, a knowledge-intensive society, and advances in information technology (NAS, 1993; Robinson, 1997). The education in science being sought is one that connects students with today's world. Each of the reform themes identified in this chapter represents conditions to which students must adapt if they are to have a high quality of life.

The importance of science/technology education for the welfare of individuals and the nation has led to the recommendation that science education policies should become a responsibility of the federal government, along with supporting relevant research (Hurd, 1997). As it stands now, there is no professional science education association or government agency that has assumed the task of designing the qualitative and empirical studies needed to provide a normative framework for education in the sciences in terms of the reform themes so far identified. A unifying synthesis of these themes is imperative if we are to effect the perceived need for revolutionary changes in science education.

In this chapter I do not claim to have identified all the problems and issues that call for a transformation of science education at this period in our nation's history. I do seek to identify major themes on which there is considerable agreement and that, unlike traditional science curricula, do not isolate students from themselves and the changing world in which they must live.

A major issue yet to be resolved is the matter of information technology in our transition to an information age. Information technology has already brought about changes in our society and human enterprises that equal or exceed those introduced by agriculture and the industrial revolution. The processing and the use of knowledge are serving to remake our personal life and the character of our society.

There are two more goals of science teaching in the middle schools. These are the development of life skills and increasing the quality of life. Though these goals are frequently mentioned in educational literature, they are seldom defined or described. In the chapter that follows these adaptive characteristics will be described.

6

Life Skills and the Quality of Life

LIFE SKILLS

Developing life skills and increasing the quality of life are frequently mentioned as goals of middle school science education but they are seldom defined. These two goals are necessary in order to provide social, cultural, and personal validity to a science curriculum that meets the needs of early adolescents.

The Carnegie Council on Adolescent Development "viewed life skills training and social supports for special attention in considering interventions that might present a wide range of damaging outcomes in education and health during childhood and adolescence" (D. Hamburg, 1990, p. i).

What are sought are intellectual and social skills that are likely to increase the adaptive capacities of students in meeting the extensive demands of a changing society. Included in these changes are those of the culture and practice of today's science, changes in the workplace, new concepts of health and wellness, and shifts in the requirements for a productive life.

The core elements of life skills for which there seems to be a consensus are listed below. The sources of the skills are from Botvin (1979 and 1980), D. Hamburg (1990), Manning (1993), Morganett (1990), Saskatchewan Newstart, Inc. (1972), and Takanishi (1993). The skills are *not* in a rank order but are considered as equal in importance.

- Capacity for cooperation
- Effective communication and ability to communicate with others
- Forming and keeping friendships
- Recognizing learning as a new form of working
- Regulating aggressive behaviors—nonviolence
- Social competence
- Conflict resolution
- Renegotiating relations with adults

- Integrating health and human services
- Cognizance of risks of using tobacco and alcohol, of substance abuse, and of sexually transmitted diseases
- Making decisions recognizing elements of risk
- Keeping your cool; stress management skills
- Developing anger management skills
- Coping with grief, death, and suicide
- School survival and success
- Self-control
- Applying problem-solving and decision-making procedures
- Able to work with others as a team
- Understanding sexuality
- Maintaining wellness, physical and mental
- Improving self-image
- Making use of criticism
- Recognizing problem situations in real life
- Recognizing the place of values, feelings, emotions, and ethics in making decisions about one's life
- Understanding nutrition
- Keeping a personal health record
- Getting acquainted with self, feeling good about self, and developing self-esteem
- Engaging in meaningful community service, Scouts, 4-H clubs, school clubs
- Participating in projects with visible outcomes
- Able to speak and be heard, knowing that one can make a difference
- Nonviolent conflict resolution
- Recognizing that today's problems of life and living will not be the same in the future
- Knowing a variety of approaches to real-life problems and situations
- Acquiring a literacy concept of the interaction of science and technology

The achievement of these life skills depends largely upon the style or mode of teaching and a social vision of science education. Specific lessons can be used to teach problem-solving and decision-making skills in a social context. An understanding of other people and their differences can be experienced through a range of teamwork activities. Some teams are all of one sex, some a mixture of boys and girls, and others a mixture of nationalities or races. Working together provides experience in forming friends, understanding other people, and relating education to the workplace where people must work together, which occurs in most positions. Other life skills, health, sexuality, and recognition of life risks can be taught directly in a context that can be lived.

QUALITY OF LIFE

Quality of life has long been an undefined goal of science education. In the context of this book it refers to the well-being of people as individuals and the supportive environments both natural and social. Science has become central to human welfare, social advancement, and economic progress. This position of science is seen as requiring a new national science policy. It is a position in which the context of science and modes of research include the physical, life, and social sciences. The report of the U.S. Congress, House Committee on Science (1998) emphasizes the importance of targeted, strategic- or product-oriented research, the findings of which can serve to improve one's health, the environment, and other aspects of life and living.

The national goal is an approach to research in the sciences that serves to ensure an advancement in the quality of life. How to translate these qualities into middle school science curricula is the task of today's curriculum developers and teachers. Although the meaning of quality of life varies with the individual, with youth and aged, with men and women, with racial minorities, and with religion and cultural backgrounds, there are elements common to all such as protecting and enhancing the natural environment and maintaining a level of health and wellness (Environmental Protection Agency, 1973). Both health and environmental studies have found a place in middle school curricula, but they are seldom taught in terms of a common vision related to the quality of life.

Quality of life as an instructional goal is based on the recognition that as we enter a knowledge-intensive age, all students will need to acquire skills related to how knowledge is obtained and managed for self and the common goal. Learning to learn, logical thinking, and other aspects of cognitive development are required for dealing with students' personal and social problems (Manning, 1993). Quality of life as an educational goal is centered on the increasing role that science/technology is playing in our lives. This concept of science education implies that science curricula ought to be centered on students and include an understanding of self and the life to which they will need to adapt. This is a scheme of science education that goes beyond the traditional discipline-based and career-oriented courses that have persisted in American schools since colonial days. What is sought is an active curriculum. This is a curriculum that can be related to life and living and keeps pace with the ethos of today's science.

Instructional goals for an emphasis on the quality of life are difficult to define, since the concept varies with each of us as we dream of ways to improve our well-being. Biologists seek conditions in which human beings and nature can exist in harmony. Social scientists look for ways in which people can live with one another to the advantage of everyone. Psychologists want to help individuals achieve a life that is satisfying and workable. Economists study ways in which societies and individuals can improve their status financially, with at least enough money not to be poverty stricken. Medical scientists seek ways to help early adolescents maintain a state of health or wellness. Artists and musicians seek to add to our aesthetic experiences that make life more pleasant. All of these attributes contribute to the emergence of a middle-level education (Manning, 1993; National Middle School Association, 1997).

Quality of life as a science education goal fades in and out as a purpose of middle school education. Part of the problem is that test makers find it difficult to assess student achievement based on the dimensions of the quality of life (Walton, 1973). Whenever this situation develops, there is a tendency to reject an educational goal because it can not be tested in traditional ways.

It should be pointed out that the quality of life as a middle school science education goal does not exist in full bloom but it is maturing, based on the experience of teachers.

7

A Lived Science Curriculum for the Middle Grades

A hundred years have passed since it was first recognized that developing adolescents should receive an education in the sciences that meets their needs. Over the years dozens of middle grades curriculum reforms have taken place. Characteristically nearly all focused on the structures and inquiry aspects of various science disciplines. From time to time the subject matter of these disciplines was reviewed and updated. The current standards movement is an example. The teaching goals implied in these science education reform movements have consistently remained internal to a discipline. In other words, the goals are unconnected with life in the real world or with the adaptive needs of early adolescents.

Today, the culture and practice of science itself are changing. "The products of science and technology have become prominent elements of the world economy and of everyday life" (National Academy of Sciences [NAS], 1993, p. v). The report emphasizes that scientific and technological progress "should demonstrably lead to improvements in the quality of life" and "in areas essential to the national well-being" (p. vi).

PURPOSE OF CHAPTER

In this chapter I focus on a synthesis of earlier chapters of this book and their meaning for a science curriculum that is basic to understanding oneself as a human being, biologically, socially, and behaviorally. The pattern of existing curricula in the sciences does not meet the adaptive needs of students for life and living in this new era of our civilization. It is also apparent that this problem cannot be resolved by focusing on the nature and practice of a discipline, or as Albert Einstein once commented, "by reasoning in the same way that caused the problem." This notion is reflected in the question often asked by students: "What good is all of this going to do me?"

54

CHARACTERISTICS OF A LIVED CURRICULUM

What is being sought today is a science curriculum that is embedded in the lives of early adolescents for dealing with personal-social problems. By contrast, traditional science courses and textbooks of today are focused on the principles, generalizations, theories and methods of scientific inquiry presumed necessary for an individual to be able to "think like a scientist" and "be like a scientist." These courses fail to foster links between the lives of early adolescents and their quality of life. The current national reform movement in science calls for a "reinvention" of traditional conceptions of science education to escape from the trap of the past. An overview of the desired transition to a lived science curriculum for early adolescents has the following characteristics.

A lived curriculum is in harmony with the new paradigm of science itself. Most research in the sciences today is focused on critical issues "confronting science and society: environmental changes and degradation; public health, particularly emergent and reemergent diseases; food and energy; education; equity, including the global maldistribution of wealth; and the public's understanding of science and technology" (Jasanoff et al., 1997, p. 2066).

A lived curriculum is personally, culturally, economically, and socially oriented. This is an approach that harmonizes with the targeted goals of scientific research. A lived curriculum is active in the context of human affairs, and goes beyond laboratory walls and the boundary of any single discipline.

A lived curriculum is interdisciplinary in nature, not only between the sciences but also between science and the social sciences and humanities. This curriculum fabric is essential for resolving personal-social problems and attaining a higher quality of life. When science knowledge is brought into human action there are also questions of values, ethics, legality, and risks to consider. An example that raises the legal and moral issues of science is that of human cloning.

A lived curriculum may also be described as making sense of science in everyday life as well as science being experienced by students. The nature of the curriculum is viewed as *active knowledge* in that it brings science into the everyday life of the student and the real world.

A lived curriculum is one in which the student develops a sense of worth and ownership. This is accomplished by organizing the curriculum around the known concerns of adolescent development that are identified in the first four chapters of this book. With these factors used as a base, the curriculum is designed in terms of projects or open-ended problems that engage the student in resolving an issue. Such a curriculum provides an opportunity for students to identify what they would like to know about themselves and others.

A lived curriculum is also seen as a fluid curriculum, a curriculum that changes incessantly in order to take advantage of new developments within the sciences or society. Most notable at the present time are Internet connections, between the student and World Wide Web, making more knowledge available for resolving human problems and issues.

In a lived curriculum, science is viewed as an instrument of service for dealing with the problems of life and living, in contrast to the concepts, principles, and theories of isolated disciplines that fail to recognize that today's science has become both humanized and socialized. During 1998 the publication *Science* (vol. 281) published a weekly essay on "science and society" written by a scientist or historian to portray science beyond discipline walls. The "standards" for a lived science curriculum are interdisciplinary and described in terms of actions for meeting human and social problems.

The art of teaching a lived science curriculum as a process of affecting every aspect of our lives will not be easy. Practically none of us as teachers or educators have been trained along these lines. A first and most important step is to form a vision of what an education in the sciences should mean for developing adolescents. The task is one of laying out a road map of a science curriculum that can serve students throughout their lives.

DEVELOPING A HUMAN LIFE SCIENCE

The 100-year effort to develop science curricula suitable to meeting the needs of the early adolescent is beginning to emerge. Past efforts have been oriented toward revising or rearranging the subject matter of traditional science disciplines such as biology, chemistry, physics, and earth science. These courses were viewed as the best preparation of students for meeting the demands of the next grade or getting into college. Students found little in these courses that they could relate to themselves and the problems of living to which they must adapt.

From the beginning, the anthropologist Margaret Mead, in her presidential talk at the American Association for the Advancement of Science, labeled the task as one focused upon the development of "a human science" (Mead, 1976).

The full meaning of a human science has yet to be fully defined. During the past 20 years many programs have emerged. More than 1,000 colleges and universities have developed new courses variously labeled "human biology," "social biology," "life science" or "human science." The NAS saw the necessity for a "drastic reorientation" of the biological sciences in the middle and high school grades with the development of a science described as "humanistic biology" (1970, p. 362). Each of these courses emphasized the study of human beings as a major focus of the biological sciences, but not in the same way. Human biology courses have replaced the frog with a human being for the study of life processes such as the digestive, muscular, excretory, circulatory, reproductive, and nervous systems. Life or human sciences represent a broader view of biology, including its social, cultural, and humanistic characteristics, a view that goes beyond the academic biology that now dominates today's textbooks. In 1998 a report by the U.S. Congress, House Committee on Science (1998) emphasized the effect of science "on elements of our lives as basic as how we live and what we eat" (p. 35).

The evolution of a life science curriculum is an attempt to provide a context for biology that can be lived, a curriculum that includes a study of life beyond the laboratory and that has meaning in the real world of life and living. Curriculum standards for a life science curriculum are those relevant to advancing the welfare of developing adolescents. Traditionally, science curriculum standards have been chosen for their value in displaying themes and structure of various science disciplines, rather than for their contribution to meeting the requirements of life as lived. Scientific inquiry as it has been taught is characteristic of the producers of science rather than of all students as consumers of science. The science-technology-society movement differs; it exemplifies an effort to orient the teaching of science in the context of human activities in the culture of our time, recognizing science as a social institution.

There are a number of sciences related to human life science: anthropology, sociology, human evolution, physiology, psychology, chemistry, physics, earth science, medicine, archaeology, human ecology, humanities, ethnology, and others. What is sought is a reconceptualization of these fields in terms of their unity for the development of a human science, with appropriate skills for everyday life as goals of instruction. During the 1930s the Progressive Education Association after six years of study proposed a human science in terms of the "interactions between the individual and the social situation." These interactions were classified as (a) personal living, (b) immediate-personal-social relationships, (c) social-civic relationships, and (d) economic relationships (Thayer, 1937, p. 27). Unfortunately the social pressures of World War II to teach "the basics" and focus on the principles and generalizations of science disciplines brought to a halt the teaching of science in terms of human affairs.

The invention of a middle grades science curriculum for developing adolescents requires an understanding of today's adolescents and of their culture as a framework for a science oriented toward human welfare. For the first time in history we can have a science that links science with human welfare as a basis for research in the sciences as well as for the invention of a modern middle school curriculum.

Development from childhood into adulthood is today different from and more complicated than that of the past. This is due to changes in family life, with both parents working; a global economy; new ways of working; new technologies for communicating; and a knowledge-intensive age. The culture and practice of science have also undergone major changes since midcentury. Computers are now viewed as the "third branch of science" ("The Third Branch of Science Debits," 1992).

We now need for the developing adolescents a road map of science education that teachers and parents understand and that makes them passionate about pursuing. Human life science as it is developing provides the subject matter that links the student with an understanding of self and the skills to facilitate one's adaptive capacities. These attributes require a curriculum formulated in terms of the student's own welfare, not the traditional structure of a discipline.

LIFE SCIENCE AND THE MIDDLE SCHOOL CURRICULUM

The proper subject of life science is humans. Developers of a science-of-life curriculum have the task of relating a generic core of concepts likely to increase the adaptive capacities of human beings throughout life. This is a view of biology as a resource from which students can draw information that will help them live meaningful lives. A middle grades curriculum in the human sciences is in a personal-social context that deals with problems of a healthy life and human affairs. Life science is concerned with what's human about human beings, as well as with understanding ourselves and our impact on the cultural and natural environments. This curriculum is seen as giving students a greater control of their lives. For a study of humans, no surrogate animal such as the frog or chimpanzee will do.

Human science is a unified view of human beings who can fulfill their obligations to society, to themselves, and to one another, a context that is seen as useful by the student. Human science can be viewed as an instrument of service. A major criticism of existing middle school science courses is that students find little they relate to. Human science is seen as an adaptive course for life in a modern society. What's more, a human science is consistent with the present culture of science itself, as a social institution.

AN INTERPRETATIVE SUMMARY

Since 1970 there have been revolutionary changes in the nature and practice of science. Scientific research is more and more focused on the national interest and problems associated with human welfare and social progress. Science is now viewed as living knowledge that citizens can use as needed. Science courses at the frontier of these changes link the sciences to the humanities and broader social conditions. The traditional discipline-bound courses now found in schools do not meet the demands of this new age.

Also beginning in the 1970s was the recognition that education in the sciences was doing little toward improving the quality of life for early adolescents, because in the middle grades it is focused on understanding the concepts, theories, facts, principles, and modes of inquiry of discrete disciplines. It has become self-evident that to meet the needs of early adolescents, science courses must be built around the developmental characteristics and problems of early adolescents, not around disciplines.

The concept of a lived curriculum unites the characteristics of today's science and the adaptive needs of developing adolescents. A lived curriculum is one oriented toward productive learning. This is a matter of transforming learning from experience into the resolution of problems concerned with human welfare and the quality of life. It is a curriculum that recognizes the socialization of today's science. The hope is that we will enter the new millennium with science as a way of life that fosters personal development, responsible citizenship and social progress and that benefits human welfare.

The lived science curriculum is action oriented in contexts that include the changing image of science as well as images of our culture. It recognizes that the needs of students are not all the same. A lived, problem-oriented curriculum provides a means for recognizing these differences; in other words it adds an element of individuality to the middle school science curriculum. A lived curriculum is recognized as a more productive way of learning.

8

The Changing Concept
of Health

An important function of a lived science curriculum for early adolescents is the development and maintenance of lifelong health. In the early chapters of this book I discussed an array of risk-taking behaviors such as substance abuse and early sex, and depression and loss of self-esteem, which became barriers to a healthy lifestyle. Health is perceived as a major component in determining the quality of life, one's personality, and achievement of human potential. This is a broader view of health than simply the absence of disease, hygiene, or the normal function of bodily organs and tissues.

A NEW VISION OF HEALTH EDUCATION

Changes taking place in today's family life, in society, and in the adaptive skills for a life none of us have as yet experienced have brought into question the meaning of health and its place in the experience of living. Health in this context is concerned with the total well-being of early adolescents and their ability to enjoy a healthy lifestyle, one that is dependent upon one's physical, mental, and social well-being. What is sought is an integrated health program. Health is more than the traditional biological concept of normal body functions and hygiene.

The aspects of health are today drawn from a number of scientific fields: physical, chemical, biological, medical, economic, geographical, social, and psychological. There are also health science professionals who specialize in different aspects of health, such as medical doctors, nurses, dentists, psychiatrists, and others. The effort today is to develop a more functional vision of health education. This vision recognizes that the task of the middle school is to teach health skills that continue throughout life and also have a potential for extending life.

NEW DIMENSIONS OF HEALTH EDUCATION

Typically health education consists of a few topics attached to general science, biology, or physical education. A major concern of the reform movement in science education is the place of health education in the middle school curriculum. The curriculum sought is one that recognizes and responds to the health problems of early adolescents.

In the 1990s, the state of adolescent health in America reached crisis proportions. Large numbers of 10- to 15-year-olds suffer from depression that may lead to suicide; they jeopardize their future by abusing illegal drugs and alcohol and by smoking; they engage in premature sexual activity; they are victims or perpetrators of violence; they lack proper nutrition and exercise. However, their glaring need for health services is largely ignored (Hechinger, 1992, p. 21). The diversity of these behaviors and their implications for health are beyond the present concepts of health education as now practiced and are inadequate for dealing with the problems Hechinger has identified.

For the past 25 years the concept of what constitutes health education has been widely debated by various groups of educators and world health organizations. Typical of their findings is that the components of health extend beyond the biological or medical aspects to include social and psychological factors. This emerging concept of health involves the total well-being of students and their quality of life, a holistic view. The changing concept of health and its themes has been studied and reported by Jan Garrard (1986).

The World Health Organization (WHO) defines health as a state of complete physical, mental, and social well-being and not merely a matter of disease or infirmity (WHO, 1978). One aspect is seen as preventative practices such as clean water, adequate housing, sanitation, environmental measures, legal control of smoking, and required vaccination of students before entering kindergarten.

The current thinking on health includes the notion of the quality of life as a whole. What does it take to become a healthy, problem-solving constructive adult? A committee sponsored by the Carnegie Corporation, after a 10-year study (A. Hamburg, 1995, p. 12), found that the key elements of an effective health education program for middle school students should enable a student to

- Find a valued place in a constructive group
- Earn a sense of worth as a person
- Achieve a reliable basis for making informed choices
- Express constructive curiosity and exploratory behavior

- Find ways of being useful to others
- Believe in a promising future with real opportunities
- Cultivate the inquiring and problem-solving habits of the mind necessary for lifelong learning and adaptability
- Learn to respect democratic values and responsible citizenship
- Build a healthy lifestyle

A synthesis of committee reports on health education suggest the following curriculum framework: (a) body health; (b) mental health; (c) environmental health; and (d) social health. It is recognized that each of these elements integrates with the others. The developers of a health curriculum also require a background in biology, psychology, sociology, anthropology, and related fields in order to develop an integrated science.

Various committees on health provide a consensus of student-centered objectives for health courses:

- Develop an ability to discriminate between fact and opinion in information related to health.
- Acquire knowledge of body systems and functions with the understanding that the growth and development of these systems follow a predictable pattern with many variations, producing unique individuals.
- Develop an understanding of the relationship between physical and emotional (mental) well-being.
- Develop an understanding of the need for proper nutrition.
- Develop the skills necessary for physical fitness.
- Develop an awareness of the relationship between human beings and their natural and social environments.
- Develop a body of knowledge about the causative agents and preventive measures relative to the common communicable diseases in the environment, and develop positive behaviors and attitudes regarding the control of such diseases.
- Develop responsible behaviors and attitudes relative to sanitation in the home and community.
- Develop an ability to make responsible decisions about alcohol, tobacco, and other drugs.
- Develop an understanding of the role of being an effective parent and of the role of the family in contemporary society.
- Develop an ability to make informed decisions concerned with sexuality.

- Acquire knowledge of the range of vocational opportunities in health and allied fields.

Committees in many countries are reviewing the present philosophy of the meaning of health. A committee located in New South Wales views health as concerned with "the total well-being of individuals and their ability to enjoy a healthy life-style" (Meyer, 1983, p. 1). The committee developed the following objectives for health studies:

- A range of physical skills that will increase body awareness and enable students to participate in a wide variety of activities of an aesthetic, recreational, and sporting nature
- A decision-making skill that will assist the individual to deal effectively with everyday life situations and contemporary health problems
- Competencies to adapt to change and cope with stress
- Positive attitudes and behavior patterns regarding fitness and choice of recreational interests
- A sense of personal and social well-being
- A responsibility for personal and social behavior
- The ability to relate effectively to others
- Expression and creativity through movement
- An awareness, understanding, and acceptance of people with physical and mental disabilities
- Positive relationships
- An appreciation of human performance
- An understanding and acceptance of individual differences
- Individual responsibility for safety
- Sport ethics, including cooperation, tolerance, and fair play
- Effective communication through physical and social activities
- The ability to function confidently and effectively as a responsible community member
- Understanding and development of a personal value (Meyer, 1983, p. 3)

A UNESCO committee on health and the biology curriculum recommended that the health objectives be student centered and include the following:

- Ability to discriminate fact and opinion in health information
- Acquisition of knowledge of body systems and functions with an understanding of normal variations producing unique individuals

- An understanding of the relationship between emotional (mental) and physical well-being
- An understanding of the need for proper nutrition
- Development of an awareness of the relationship of human beings and the natural and social environment (*Connect*, 1998, pp. 1–4; UNESCO, n.d., p. 13)

The present reform movement in science education emphasizes science for all. The health education movement is in the process of making wellness one of the major educational goals. There are problems in and out of school that are yet to be fully considered. It is obvious that much of a student's health is influenced by parents before and after children enter school. Nutrition and medical care are functions of the home as well as of the school. Poverty restricts much of what can be done to insure student health. At the same time, many parents do not have a concept of what health as an instructional goal is about. The U.S. Department of Education is sponsoring a series of national programs to encourage parents to become more involved in education (*Community Update*, ongoing monthly issues, free). The pursuit of healthy individuals is seen as requiring a partnership with the home and community, and an active involvement of parents.

THE SIGNIFICANCE OF HEALTH EDUCATION REFORM

Since the turn of this century changes in family structures, in the workplace, and in the daily life of students and a limited view of health education have resulted in student health problems that youths have never faced before. The National Middle School Association (NMSA) believes that there is a serious need to "develop programs, and policies that foster health, wellness, and safety" (NMSA, 1995, p. 11). Typically adolescents view health as simply "not being sick," or the absence of disease. Unfortunately too many health courses in middle schools have the same limitations.

The substance of this chapter has been about efforts to conceptualize the elements of health education. The modern focus on health education includes perspectives on the personal, social, and psychological aspects of health. The health curriculum in the middle school initiates one's health status for a lifetime. Health studies are the major component of a lived curriculum. The concept of health and what it means to be healthy has undergone major changes in the past 20 years and likely other changes will emerge in the future.

9

Preparing for Life: A Science of Ourselves

The changing views of health as an educational goal establish a new rationale for the development of middle school science curricula. The purpose of this chapter is to identify major learning concepts of health as they relate to the quality of life.

Criteria used for the selection of subject matter were derived from (a) early adolescent concerns and interests about self and others, (b) perceived rationale of the middle school education, (c) maladaptive behaviors currently associated with adolescent development, and (d) recognition of recommendations of the national reports on improving the quality of American education.

The curriculum is viewed as a "human life science" and draws upon the following fields of study for subject matter concepts: anthropology, biology, biogeography, medical sciences, psychology, sociology, and technology. The integrative structure connecting these fields consists of human beings and their adaptive characteristics: biological, behavioral, social, and historical. Course topics are not viewed as complete nor are they intended to be. The curriculum being an introduction to life science, the primary intent is to raise the students' level of awareness about themselves.

The final organization of the course should be in terms of problems and issues that provide the personal involvement of students in their own learning and that get students to apply their learning directly to understanding their own behavior. A certain amount of redundancy should be built into the course to convey to students the notion that problems are interconnected and will be viewed in new ways as one learns more. The problems and issues to be dealt with should be those that arise from real-life situations and should be in the context of the cultural and social conditions that generated them.

The course is to be supplemented with an almost daily series of laboratory-type experiments, exercises, observations, and community studies that directly involve the student, such as perceptual experiments, memory exercises, determining factors that influence one's heart rate and blood pressure, making surveys, and conducting polls. A substantial number of these activities should be collaborative endeavors by small groups of students; using this approach will have the extra advantage of adding to the socialization of the student.

A MIDDLE GRADES LIFE SCIENCE CURRICULUM

The following outline identifies curriculum principles for the development of a life science curriculum for the middle grades. All of these principles are broadly focused on the betterment of the individual. The list is not absolute and never will be. As teachers we need to recognize that we are living in a period of rapid changes in family life, in society, and in advances of the culture and practice of science. All of these changes have implications for the adaptive needs of individuals.

    I. Getting to Know Ourselves: What Kind of a Creature Are We?
  - Study ourselves and other people and learn what it is to be human.
  - Some animals are superior to humans in one or more ways, such as in seeing, hearing, running, jumping, swimming, and longevity.
  - Humans are superior to all other animals in their capacity to learn, adapt and make choices, use language and tools, and control their environment.
  - Physical characteristics that distinguish human beings from other animals are brain, posture, limbs, skull, teeth, and rate of growth and development.
  - The physical, social, and emotional growth of males and females during puberty and adolescence is a human trait.
  - Social/cultural characteristics distinguish human beings from other animals, for example, the formation of cities, the development of agriculture and domestication of animals, technological innovations, and generating new knowledge through observation and experiment.
  - Ways in which people are all alike and also ways in which each person is different from everybody else define the meaning of personality.

   II. People Have a Long History on Earth
  - The capacity of human beings to adapt to changing conditions on the earth have enabled them to survive. Animals that failed to adapt to changes on the earth did not survive.

- Human beings today are a single biological species with common physical characteristics, but with distinctive behavioral and social characteristics.
- There are varieties of people called races who tend to have common physical characteristics.
- All human beings have many characteristics in common yet there are no two people on earth who are exactly alike: normal and abnormal human beings.
- Genetic factors influence ways in which people differ; for example, albinism, baldness, cystic fibrosis, sickle-cell anemia, blood types, near- and farsightedness, eye color, and shape of ear lobes.
- Ethnic or cultural factors sometimes make people seem different: food preferences, clothes, language, music preferences, native dances, hairstyles.
- Cultural, physical, technological, and environmental factors influence how people adapt today and how they respond to changes in their immediate technological and cultural environments.
- Connecting students to Internet links and Web sites enhances life experiences.
- Identify careers that are related to the study of human beings, their origins, characteristics, and survival.

III. Human Life Cycle
- How early adolescents become adapted to life.
- The human life cycle from conception to old age: characteristics of different age groups of human beings, longevity changes.
- Early adolescent development; what to expect in the next few years. Signs of physical maturity including growth rates.
- The reproductive process and what it means for individuals and society. Diseases that may result from sexual contacts: venereal diseases and AIDS and how they may be prevented.
- Patterns of growth and development influenced by heredity and by social and environmental factors: nutrition, exercise, poverty, disease, and glandular functions (pituitary).
- Behavioral and social changes in early adolescence; finding one's place in social groups: friendships, family, peers, boy-girl relationships.
- Resolving personal problems or conflicts: loneliness, depression, and death of a friend. Where to get the best help or advice on conflicts.
- Care of the body during early adolescence: skin, nutrition, exercise, and sleep.

- Time to begin planning for a career and what is involved: developing an interest, finding out what people do, and requirements for schooling. The information age places new demands on career preparation.

IV. How We Learn About People and the World

- Our sense organs receive information that helps us to adapt to changes in our environment.
- Our sense organs are adapted to receiving specific stimuli within certain limits: eyes, ears, taste, smell, balance, and skin (heat, cold, touch, pain).
- Extending the limits of our senses through technology: eyeglasses, telescopes, and listening devices.
- What our senses tell us and don't tell us: perception as the interpretation of stimuli. Advantages of two ears and two eyes. Factors that influence perception: culture, awareness, distractions, illusions, attention, color blindness. Influence of drugs and alcohol on perception.
- The world without one or more of our senses: blindness, deafness. How people can adapt to the loss of a sense: sign language, Braille, hearing aids.
- Care and safety practices for our senses: glasses, effects of loud noise on hearing, sun and eyes, chemicals, and so on. Dangers from an impaired sense of smell and taste.
- Disorders of the eye—astigmatism, cataracts, cross-eyes, glaucoma, inflammation of eyes and lids, near- and farsightedness and what can be done. Disorders of the ear—ringing, impacted wax, loss of balance, and what can be done.

V. Learning and Remembering

- Human beings adapt to the natural and social worlds principally by their ability to acquire and use knowledge.
- Human beings differ from other animals in their greater capacity to learn.
- Most of what we learn depends upon the effort we make to acquire information. Effort depends upon whether we want to learn something or not (motivation and drive) and how much we value learning.
- Some of the things we do are not learned (reflexes, instincts). Compare instinctive behavior in animals with that of human beings.
- There are different ways of learning (acquiring skills, conditioning, growing up in a culture). How do animals acquire skills? Learning and memory in human beings are influenced by needs, wishes, and attitudes.

- Ways we can improve learning and remembering: by use, attitude, and making connections and reviewing and developing study skills.
- Conditions that can lessen our ability to learn: alcohol, drugs, injuring the brain, genetic factors, and language deficiencies.
- Where it all happens: the nervous system and how each part functions.
- Ways of protecting the nervous system from injury: use of helmets and seat belts. Some disorders and diseases of the nervous system: shingles, epilepsy, neuritis.
- Learning and careers. Whatever career we choose means we will need to know more or be more skillful than most people. Learning to learn and the utilization of knowledge have become major educational goals.

VI. Language and Communication
- Language is unique to human beings and is a basic adaptive characteristic.
- Language has made culture possible and differentiates humankind from all other animals.
- Language connects us to our perceptual world and makes possible the transfer of information from one person to another.
- Language shapes our individual and collective behavior, helping to identify the personalities of individuals and their relationship to other human beings.
- Each subject taken in school adds to the growth of our language ability and provides a larger basis for thinking and improving our social development.
- Countries and people with a limited command of language are unable to benefit from modern science and technology with the result that they tend to live in poverty.
- Communication may be verbal or written. Written language developed in civilizations long after verbal language and makes it possible to preserve our thoughts.
- In addition to using oral and written language, people convey messages by means of facial expressions, body movements, symbols, pictures, art forms, and gesture.
- Communicative behavior in nonhuman animals is typically limited to alarm and mating sounds and takes the form of screams, growls, whistles, dancing, pounding chest, making faces, body postures, flattening ears against head, or showing teeth.
- Talking by humans depends upon a larynx to generate sounds and a throat and tongue to shape sounds. As the larynx develops

with age our voice changes, especially during adolescence and old age.

- The current information age, with modern technology for storing and transmitting messages, makes language an increasingly important component of personal development and socialization.
- Disorders of speech: stuttering, stammering, lisping, and other problems. Drugs and alcohol can affect the way we speak.
- Art, music, symbols, and mathematics are patterns of communication.
- Nearly every career has a special vocabulary or language of its own that one must learn to be successful in that career and to be able to communicate with others in the same field.

VII. Knowing and Deciding
- The basis of human adaptability is our capacity to put knowledge to work in meeting the challenges of life and deciding on a course of action.
- Possessing a lot of knowledge does not assure wise actions; the knowledge must be reliable and we must understand how to use it appropriately.
- Science through repeated observations, experimentation, verification, and consensus is a reliable source of information. To identify reliable sources of information one must be able to distinguish evidence from propaganda, probabilities from certainties, questions from pseudoquestions, rational beliefs from superstitions, science from quackery, data from assertions, science from myth and folklore, known from what is not known, credible from incredible, sense from nonsense, fact from fiction, and theory from dogma.
- It is not likely that everyone will view a problem in the same way. Using the same information, we and other people may reach different conclusions. Decisions may also be influenced by stereotypes, cultural traditions, moral beliefs, personal values, ethics, how data are best interpreted, an unclear statement of a problem, perceptions of information, peer pressures, how statistics are represented, unrecognized variables, and not asking enough questions. Some decisions are biased by trade-offs, bandwagon effects, personal wishes, a desire for a quick answer, use of emotionally charged words, or an inadequate vocabulary. Other decisions may be risky and we are likely to regret them later on when we have more information.
- Since one person can not know everything, it is sometimes best

to allow an expert, a specialist, an authority, or someone with more experience to help us make a decision, for example, a medical doctor, dentist, engineer, scientist, parent, coach or trainer. Other sources of information include libraries, databanks, textbooks, the Internet and what we have learned or experienced in our own life. The use of surveys, polls, case histories, are sometimes used to help make decisions.

- We must be aware of the use and limitations of modern information technology, such as the computer, in decision making.
- Making good decisions is not always possible for people whose judgment is influenced by drugs and alcohol, or who have injuries or diseases of the brain.
- Making decisions as a group can be influenced by degrees of cooperation, compliance, competition, conflict, compromise, and prejudice.
- Being smart in life is to be a good decision maker using reliable information and avoiding risks.

VIII. Nutrition
- Nutrition is a basic factor in promoting good health.
- All living organisms require a continuous supply of energy for optimal health. Most life forms are dependent on green plants and their capacity to transform energy in ways useful to the plants and animals.
- Food choices we make influence bone and muscle growth and their strength.
- Our body requires a variety of proteins, carbohydrates, and fats, in proper ratios to achieve optimal health. In addition, chemical elements are also essential, for example, magnesium, iron, iodine, fluorine, calcium, sodium, potassium, and phosphorous. Additional substances such as dietary fiber, vitamins, and water are also a necessary part of proper nutrition. Food requirements change from one phase of our life to another.
- A proper balance of food substances (good eating habits) is essential for a healthy life. Overnutrition results in excess fat or obesity, which in turn lowers mobility and may in time result in heart failure or may influence our susceptibility to disease. Undernutrition damages the body, lowers our energy level, reduces our ability to resist diseases, may result in dental caries, and may otherwise harm our body. Poor eating habits sometimes result in allergies, hives, upset stomach, indigestion, or constipation. Careless handling of food may also cause illness,

such as dysentery, salmonella, ptomaine poisoning, or botulism.
- How food is prepared can change its value to the body such as in overcooking, improper storage, or lack of freshness.
- The digestive system is a series of specialized organs that process the food we eat so that it may be useful to the body.
- Today's rapid growth of the world population is increasing the need for an adequate supply of food.
- Agricultural specialists work to improve the production of food and its nutritional quality, taste or flavor, and shipping characteristics.
- Careers related to the raising of food and its proper use and preparation are on the increase.

IX. Health, Hygiene, and Safety
- State of health is an expression of success or failure in responding adaptively to the challenges of life and living. Healthy behavior has biological, social, cultural, and psychological dimensions that interact in a tangled web.
- Modern medicine is an adaptive procedure based upon research and experience in contrast to myth, superstition, folklore, and drug advertisements.
- Achieving optimal health and well-being is a continuing endeavor extending beyond the present and going on throughout life. The direction and practices of healthy behavior are for the most part under the control of each individual.
- Physical fitness requires a balance of exercise, sleep, rest, nutrition, and relaxation in a favorable environment.
- Good mental health requires one to keep mentally active, have fun, and control stress; be with others; develop positive attitudes; adjust to changes in life; curb fear, jealousy, and anger; form life goals; take time for relaxation and recreation.
- Body warnings that our health is not what it should be: temperature changes, pain, headaches, upset stomach, changes in heart rate, sleeplessness, changes in mood.
- How disease organisms enter the body: nose, lungs, skin, and intestines.
- The immune system as a bodily defense.
- How diseases are spread: food, water, coughing, sneezing, direct contact, and insects.
- Animals that carry diseases to human beings: mosquitoes, flies, ticks, lice, fleas.
- Body disorders: upset stomach, glands (diabetes, goiter), joints, allergies, epilepsy, chronic bronchitis.

- Irregular cell growth as a disease: cancer, tumors, warts.
- Preventing diseases: cleanliness, vaccination, avoiding exposure, first aid.
- Playing it safe and preventing injuries: bicycle and auto safety, home safety, protecting self from other people, using emergency help (phone 911), seeking medical help, obeying signals, recognizing poisons, using first aid procedures, purchasing health insurance.
- Helping to develop a healthy environment: public and community health, pollution control (air, water, soil, chemical sprays).
- Diseases you can't do much about: genetic diseases, birth abnormalities.
- Unhealthy conditions you can do something about: drugs, alcohol, and tobacco use.
- Where to find reliable information on health when needed: choosing a medical advisor.
- Careers in health and medical fields.

X. Human Beings as Social Animals
  - Human adaptive behaviors in the context of society or culture include seeking companionship, love, and identity in group settings such as family, friends, organizations, and institutions.
  - Cities and urban living have emerged from human efforts to benefit from the advantages of group association and cooperative efforts in sustaining life and social development.
  - Human beings have been successful as social animals to the extent they have been able to control and manage their natural and biological environments by such means as the domestication of plants and animals, control of energy resources, innovation of new technologies, and dissemination of information.
  - The natural environment on which we must depend for our existence is being jeopardized by increases in population and poor management, which are destroying the food capacity of land; pollution of air, water, and soil; the overuse of mineral resources and the potential of radiation.
  - Social environments may become less desirable and threaten the quality of human life through crime, drugs, alcohol, political restrictions, poverty, and people failing to cooperate.
  - Rules or laws are sometimes needed to strengthen the cooperative efforts of groups to maintain a safe social environment and coordinate the efforts of groups.
  - Not all cultural groups adapt to their natural social environments in the same manner.

- As social animals all human beings are expected to contribute to the common good by working, sharing, serving, and cooperating.

SUMMARY

The life science course should be planned for a 3-year sequence. Topics presented should be broadly related to the maturity level of early adolescents. Questions related to the ethical and legal aspects of science are best dealt with in later years. Many aspects of life science change at irregular times due to new discoveries. The placement of a topic is best at the age level where students ask the most questions on an issue. It should be recognized that standardized tests of student achievement in the life sciences do not at present exist. The nature of human life science should be carefully explained to parents each year.

These health principles identified were abstracted from hundreds of articles on adolescent needs over the last decade. They provide a base for initiating new curricula for the middle school.

10

What's Next?

THE PROBLEM

In the preface of this book it was noted that 2,000 years ago Aristotle was concerned with the developmental problems of early adolescents. After visiting schools in Athens to learn how education might be improved he concluded:

> There are doubts concerning the business of education since all people do not agree on those things which they would have a child taught, both with respect to improvement in virtue and a happy life; nor is it clear whether the object of it should be to improve the reason or rectify the morals. From the present mode of education we cannot determine with certainty to which men incline, whether to instruct a child in which will be useful to him in life, or what tends to virtue, or what is excellent; for all these things have their separate defenders (trans. 1964, p. 268).

One hundred years ago, major changes were taking place in the social structure of the United States, as the nation moved from an agrarian to an industrial society. The movement led families to move from the country to cities. One result was the inability of many early adolescents to adapt to the new conditions of living. The Committees of Ten, Twelve, and Fifteen of the National Education Society (1894) recommended that early adolescents should be assigned to special schools. In the following years these schools became the junior high school (Grades 7, 8, 9) and later the middle school (Grades 6, 7, 8).

In the 1970s it was again recognized that developing adolescents were not getting the sort of education they needed in order to adapt to our rapidly changing society, new family structures, and an information age. Over the past 20 years there have been extensive studies of the problems of early adolescent development: Adey, Bliss, Head, & Shayer (1987), Carnegie Council on Adolescent Development (1995), Chadwick & Heaton (1996), Feldman & Elliott (1990), Graubard (1971), Hargreaves, Earl, & Ryan (1996), Hechinger (1992), National Research Council (1993), Takanishi (1993). One can conclude that it has taken 2,000 years to recognize that a middle school science curriculum should be a product of the adaptive "needs of early adolescents" and not that of the structure of science disciplines. The modern search for a new vision of science education was proposed by Hurd (1984).

SCIENCE EDUCATION—ROAD MAPS FOR CHANGE

A new curriculum must be invented. Efforts to reform science education over the past 100 years have been simply a matter of updating the concepts, principles, and theories related to various disciplines. Again, as Albert Einstein once commented, you cannot solve a problem by thinking in the same terms that caused the problem. With a new vision of what early adolescent development should be about, the source of subject matter for a new curriculum comes from the collective knowledge about human beings from whatever disciplines now house this knowledge. This is likely to be best accomplished by a team of biologists, psychologists, sociologists, anthropologists, selected medical specialists, early adolescents, and experienced middle school teachers.

Another road map to consider is the professionalism of middle school science teachers. For the past 100 years the professional education of teachers for the middle grades has been that of an elementary or a secondary school teacher. The need for a special preparation of science teachers for particular grade levels has been debated since 1839, when Horace Mann declared that teachers should be specially prepared for different grade levels (Cruickshank et al., 1996, p. 3).

A central task of teacher education for the middle grades is to first provide a candidate with a vision of early adolescent development. The professionalism of middle school teachers is a lifelong task constantly fomented by changes in the adaptive needs of early adolescents caused by new developments in society, the economy, science/technology, communication, and research on learning.

Teachers are central to a science education reform. This task includes the ability to transmit suggested standards into sound pedagogical principles (National Institute for Educational Research, 1997, p. 105). The National Commission on Teaching and America's Future (1996) points out that good teaching is more important than ever before in the nation's history. The commission also noted that "a caring, competent, and qualified teacher for every child is the most important ingredient in today's educational reform" (p. vi).

Over the past decade the NAS has taken an active interest in the preparation of science teachers for the first time in its 150-year history. Bruce Alberts, president of the academy, points out the "need for radical changes in preservice science teacher preparation. In fact, we are faced with the need for radical changes in two recalcitrant populations: science faculty who teach undergraduate science courses and education faculty teaching methods courses and supervising field experiences" (NRC, 1997, p. 191). The NAS recognizes that our increasing technological society requires that the quality of teacher preparation demands new guidelines, both for preservice and inservice (Gilford & Tenenbaum, 1990). The NAS (1996) overviewed a number of university programs for science-teacher preparation that involved both scientists and educators.

The Directorate for Education and Human Resources of the National Science Foundation has established a division for the education of teachers. "The ultimate goal is to achieve excellence in the preparation of future teachers—teachers who are knowledgeable of the content areas and in the practice of teaching; creative and enthusiastic, and dedicated to lifelong learning" (Directorate for Education, 1996, p. ii). By 1996 the Directorate for Education had funded more than 120 colleges and universities for the preparation of teachers by means of undergraduate integrated science programs (p. iv). The federal government supports a wide variety of programs devoted to the development of professional teachers. The quality of these programs has yet to be determined (*Achieving the Goals*, 1994, p. 145).

The National Board for Professional Teaching Standards (1996) is seeking to prepare teachers for a vision of science that focuses on the human contexts of science, a context that promotes the use of science in making wise decisions, in the understanding of self, and in participation in civic life. The key to success in realizing these goals rests with teachers in the middle grades who know, accept, and believe in the new policies and perspectives for science education in these grades.

The Carnegie Forum on Education and the Economy (1986) stresses that the effectiveness of schooling rests upon recognizing that "the focus of schooling must shift from teaching to learning, from passive acquisition of facts and routines to the application of ideas to problems" (p. 25). The teacher's function is to help students obtain the best way of achieving these goals. Teachers state that there is little in their university courses in either science or education that assists them in the task of enabling students to adapt to the information age, the culture and practice of today's science, changes in the economy, and an understanding of the common culture. The Carnegie Forum on Education and the Economy (1986) viewed the problem of the professional education of science teachers as being in need of a complete "rebuilding," and stated that it must be continuous throughout their lifetime because of "the continually changing nature of the subject matter" (p. 45).

Efforts to bring about a national reform in science education have been under way for the past 140 years. Herbert Spencer in his book *Education: Intellectual, Mind, and Physical* (1860), raised the question, "What knowledge is of most worth?" He noted:

> Men read books on this topic, and attend lectures on that subject; decide that their children be instructed in these branches of knowledge, and shall not be instructed in those; and under the guidance of mere custom or liking, or prejudice; without ever considering the enormous importance of determining in some rational way what things are really most worth learning. (p. 11)

A symposium sponsored by the National Research Council (NRC) in 1996 sought to "define and to articulate policies to enhance investment in human capital" (NRC, 1996a, pp. vii, viii). The participants of the symposium define a range of reform policies and associated research that call for "improving America's schools" but they do not, as a group, state agreed-upon policies. The reader will note that the majority of educational policies are related to economic changes and that a major purpose of education in the 21st century is to develop more productive students.

THE NEED FOR MIDDLE SCHOOL SCIENCE CURRICULUM CENTERS

Thomas Jefferson, when vice president of the United States in 1798, noted that little practical science was being taught in the schools at any grade level. He viewed science "as keys to the treasures of nature . . . hands must be trained to use them wisely." Jefferson enlisted his friend DuPont de Nemours, a medical doctor and minister of agriculture in France, to survey the teaching of science in American schools at all grade levels and to make recommendations for improvement. De Nemours reported that teachers said they had no textbooks that related science to practical affairs or that enhanced progress of the country as a developing nation (de Nemours, 1923, pp. 55 and 159). The U.S. Congress refused to grant money to develop science curricula with the comment that schools and the church belong to the local community.

After 300 years the desired science curriculum for middle schools has yet to emerge. This science curriculum would be portrayed as an instrument of democracy, of social and economic progress for the nation, and of the education of all students as productive members of society. It is beyond the capacity of local communities to make a landmark study of American society, of the culture of today's science, and of unlocking of our future in order to formulate a science curriculum for the 21st century. Bruce Alberts, president of the NAS notes: "The presidential candidates like to say how each community knows what's best for its children. But it took the NAS four years of agony to come up with these [science] standards, so it's beyond me how they expect local communities to do it on their own" (Alberts, 1996).

What the nation needs is one or more public agencies or institutions consisting of individuals who know the social history of science/technology, are aware of the adaptive needs of developing adolescents, and comprehend the revolution taking place in information technology and its potential for advancing learning. As it stands now, this is not the expertness of teachers who have neither the educational background nor time to develop curricula for a world they have yet to experience. Another dimension of the current science education reform movement is that of parents. While they are critical of the science education they had when they attended school, they do not propose changes consistent with the advancements of science, social changes, and a knowledge-intensive society. Typically parents advocate science courses that are simply "more rigorous."

The National Science Resources Center, representing the Smithsonian Institution, the NAS, the National Academy of Engineering, and the Institute of Medicine, has produced a volume focused exclusively on curriculum materials and the resources for teaching middle school science (National Science Resources Center, 1998). The materials are not presented within the context of a specific core science curriculum that is based on the stated needs of developing adolescents.

The National Center on Education and the Economy (1997) has reported new middle school standards in science and applied learning. These standards take into account previous publications on school science standards, such as those of the American Association for the Advancement of Science and the National Research Council.

The Carnegie Council on Adolescent Development devoted nearly a decade to the study of adolescent development for a new century. The council provides educational answers to observations made by Aristotle 2,000 years ago on the nature of adolescent development.

A NATIONAL CURRICULUM CENTER

It has become evident that there is a need to establish a permanent national center for curriculum development in school sciences. About every 20 to 30 years, efforts are made to improve the performance of schools and update the subject matter in science courses. Traditional goals are restated and standardized tests are updated. Usually a science education reform movement lasts about 3 years. The present reform period has been ongoing for nearly 30 years with few results. The movement is now propelled by the National Middle School Association (1998).

Part of the reform problem is that there is no one at the helm, no permanent public agency to synthesize, interpret, and serve as a clearinghouse on policies, issues, gaps in research, and the development of tests consistent with the emerging goals of science education at different levels of schooling.

The center should be financially supported by the federal government and staffed by scholars drawn from many science disciplines, psychologists, sociologists, policy analysts, historians, and other specialists as needed. The complexity of science curriculum development is influenced by changes in the adaptive needs of students, an information age, changes in the culture and practices of science/technology, new modes of communication, and the pace of social changes. It is estimated that the changes in our society, economy, and lifestyle have been greater over the past 100 years than in the previous 1,000 years. These changes make professional teacher development a lifelong enterprise.

References

Abelson, P. H. (1995, November 10). Editorial, *Science, 270*(5238), 895.

Achieving the Goals: Goal 4. Teacher Education and Professional Development. (1994). Washington, DC: U.S. Government Printing Office.

Adey, P. P., Bliss, J., Head, J., & Shayer, M. (Eds.). (1987). *Adolescent development and school science.* Bristol, PA: Falmer Press.

Alberts, B. (1996, March 8). Rough going. *Science, 271*(5254) (Unpaginated).

Alexander, W. M. (1964). *The junior high school: A changing view.* Washington, DC: National Association of Secondary School Principals.

Alexander, W. M. (1978). How fares the middle school movement? *Middle School Journal, 9*(3).

Alexander, W. M., & George, P. S. (1981). *The exemplary middle school.* New York: Holt, Rinehart and Winston.

Alexander, W. M., & Williams, E. L. (1965). Schools for the middle years. *Educational Leadership, 23*(3).

Alexander, W. M., Williams, E. L., Comptom, M., Hines, V. A., & Prescott, D. (1968). *The emergent middle school.* New York: Basic Books.

American Association for the Advancement of Science (AAAS). (1993). *Benchmarks for science literacy: Project 2061.* New York: Oxford University Press.

Aristotle. (trans. 1964). *Politics* and *Poetics* (B. Jewett & S. H. Butcher, Trans.). New York: Heritage Press.

Armstrong, J., Mayer, K., & Wilkins, J. (1986). *Fifty-state survey of middle/junior high school science initiatives and issues.* Denver, CO: Education Commission of the States.

Ayres, L. P. (1909). *Laggards in our schools.* New York: Russell Sage Foundation.

Barnett, L. J., Handel, G., & Weser, H. (1968). *The schools in the middle: Divided opinion on dividing schools.* New York: Center for Urban Education.

Batezel, W. G. (1968). The middle school: Philosophy program, organization. *The Clearing House, 42*(8).

Benson, P. L., Sharma, A. R., & Roenlkepartain, E. C. (1994). *Growing up adopted: A portrait of adolescents and their families.* Minneapolis, MN: Search Institute.

Bezilla, R. (Ed.). (1993). *American youth in the 1990s.* Princeton, NJ: George H. Gallup International Institute.

Blosser, P. E. (1983, October, November, December). Teaching science to middle school students. Parts 1–3. *School Science and Mathematics, 83*(6, 7, 8).

Botvin, G. J. (1979). *Life skill training: Student guide.* New York: Smithfield Press.

Botvin, G. J. (1980). *Life skills training: Year 3 booster curriculum*. New York: Cornell University Medical College.

Briggs, T. H. (1927). *The junior high school*. Boston: Ginn.

Brod, P. (1966). The middle school: Trends toward its adoption. *Clearinghouse, 40*(6).

Brooks, K. C. (1978). The middle school: A national survey. *Middle School Journal, 9*(2).

Carnegie Commission. (1994). *Enabling the future: Linking science and technology to societal goals*. New York: Carnegie Commission on Science, Technology, and Government.

Carnegie Council on Adolescent Development. (1989). *Turning points: Preparing American youth for the 21st century*. New York: Carnegie Corporation of New York.

Carnegie Council on Adolescent Development. (1995). *Great transitions: Preparing adolescents for a new century*. New York: Author.

Carnegie Forum on Education and the Economy. (1986). *A nation prepared: Teachers for the 21st century*. New York: Author.

Chadwick, B. A., & Heaton, T. B. (1996). *Statistical handbook on adolescents in America*. Phoenix, AZ: Oryx Press.

Cohen, K. C. (Ed.). (1997). *Internet links for science education: Student-scientists partnerships*. New York: Plenum Press.

Collins, W. A. (Ed.). (1984). *Development during middle childhood: The years from six to twelve*. Washington, DC: National Academy Press.

Commission for a Nation of Lifelong Learners. (1997). *Vision for the 21st century*. Albany, NY: Regents College.

Committee of Ten, Twelve, Fifteen. (1894). *NEA reports*. New York: American Book.

Committee on Science, Engineering, and Public Policy. (1993). *Science, technology, and the federal government: National goals for a new era*. Washington, DC: National Academy Press.

Compton, M. F. (1968). Alternatives to the status quo. *Theory into Practice, 7*(3).

Conant, J. B. (1960). *Education in the junior high school years*. Princeton, NJ: Educational Testing Service.

Connect. (1998). *Health promoting schools* (Vol. 2). Paris: UNESCO.

Cruickshank, D. R., et al. (1996). *Preparing America's teachers*. Bloomington, IN: Phi Delta Kappa Educational Foundation.

Daley, W. M. (1997). *Statistical abstracts of the United States, 1997*. Washington, DC: Department of Commerce.

de Nemours, D. (1923). *National education in the United States*. Newark, DE: University of Delaware Press.

DeVita, J. C., Pumerantz, P., & Wilkiow, L. B. (1970). *The effective middle school*. West Nyack, NY: Parker Publishing House.

Dick, H. (Ed.). (1955). *Selected writings of Francis Bacon*. New York: Random House.

Directorate for Education and Human Resources. Division of Undergraduates.

(1996). *Teacher preparation and NSF collaborative for excellence in teacher preparation.* Arlington, VA: National Science Foundation.

Dorman, G. (1987). *Improving middle-grade schools: A framework for action.* Chapel Hill, NC: Center for Early Adolescents.

Douglass, A. A. (1916). *The junior high school.* Bloomington, IL: Public School.

Educational Research Council of Greater Cleveland. (1960). *Junior high school leadership conference 1960: A summary report.* Cleveland, OH: Author.

Eichhorn, D. (1980). Middle school developmental age grouping: A needed consideration. In D. R. Steer (Ed.), *The emerging adolescent: Characteristics and educational implications.* Fairborn, OH: National Middle School Association.

Environmental Protection Agency. (1973). *The quality of life: A potential new tool for decision makers.* Washington, DC: Author.

Feldman, S. S., & Elliott, G. R. (Eds.). (1990). *At the threshold: The developing adolescent.* Cambridge, MA: Harvard University Press.

Franklin, B. (1743). *A proposal for promoting useful knowledge among the British plantations in America.* (From a photocopy of Franklin's original manuscript, courtesy of Yale University Library.)

Freshman characteristics and attitudes. (1984). *Chronicle of Higher Education 27*(21), 13.

Frymier, J., Cornbleth, C., Donmoyer, R., Gansneder, B., Jeter, J., Klein, M., Schwab, M., & Alexander, W. (1984). *One hundred good schools: A report of the Good Schools Project.* West Lafayette, IN: Kappa Delta Pi.

Gallup International Institute, G. H. (1991). *The Gallup survey on teenage suicide.* Princeton, NJ: Author.

Garrard, J. (1986). Health education and science education: Changing roles, common goals? *Studies in Science Education, 13,* 1–26.

Gatewood, T. E., Dilg, C. A., & Charles, A. (1975). *The middle school we need.* Washington, DC: Association for Supervision and Curriculum Development.

George, P. S. (Ed.). (1977). *The middle school: A look ahead.* Fairborn, OH: National Middle School Association.

George, P. S. (1983). *The theory "Z" school: Beyond effectiveness.* Columbus, OH: National Middle School Association.

George, P. S., & Oldoker, L. (1985). *Evidence for the middle schools.* Columbus, OH: National Middle School Association.

Gilford, D. M., & Tenenbaum, E. (Eds.). (1990). *Pre-college science and mathematics teachers: Monitoring supply, demand, and quality.* Washington, DC: National Academy Press.

Glickman, D. (1998, October 28). Obesity in kids at epidemic level. *San Jose Mercury News,* p. 11A.

Goodman, P. (1964). *Compulsory mis-education.* New York: Horizon Press.

Grambs, J. D., Noyce, C. G., Patterson, F., & Robertson, J. C. (1961). *The junior high school we need.* Washington, DC: Association for Supervision and Curriculum Development.

Graubard, S. R. (Ed.). (1971, Fall). Twelve to sixteen: Early adolescence [Entire issue]. *Daedalus, 100*(4). Richmond, VA: American Academy of Arts and Sciences.

Gruhn, W. T., & Douglas, H. R. (1971). *The modern junior high school* (3rd ed.). New York: The Ronald Press.

Guttmacher Institute. (1994). *Sex and America's teenager.* New York: Author.

Hamburg, A. (1995). *A developmental strategy to prevent lifelong damage.* New York: Carnegie Corporation of New York.

Hamburg, D. A. (1990). *Life skills training: Preventive interventions for young adolescents.* Washington, DC: Carnegie Council on Adolescent Development.

Hargreaves, A. (1986). *Two cultures of schooling: The case of the middle schools.* New York: Falmer Press.

Hargreaves, A., Earl, L., & Ryan, J. (1996). *Schooling for change: Reinventing education for early adolescents.* Bristol, PA: Falmer Press.

Hart, L. (1969). *The classroom disaster.* New York: Teachers College Press.

Hechinger, F. M. (1992). *Fateful choices: Healthy youth for the 21st century.* New York: Hill and Wang.

Hentoff, N. (1967). *Our children are dying.* New York: Viking Press.

Holmes, B. C., Kaplan, A. S., Lang, E. J., & Card, J. J. (1991). *National health interview survey of children, 1988: A user's guide to the machine-readable files and documentation.* Los Altos, CA: Sociometrics Corporation.

Holt, J. (1964). *How children fail.* New York: Dell.

H.R. 2884. *School-to-work opportunities act of 1994.* Washington, DC: U.S. Congress.

H.R. 4078. *Workforce readiness act of 1992.* Washington, DC: U.S. Congress.

Hueftle, S. J., Rakow, S. J., & Welch, W. W. (1983). *Images of science: A summary of results from the 1981–82 National Assessment of Science.* Minneapolis: University of Minnesota Education and Research Center.

Hurd, P. D. (1958). Science literacy: Its meaning for American schools. *Educational Leadership, 17,* 13–16.

Hurd, P. D. (1970). *New curriculum perspectives for junior high school science.* Belmont, CA: Wadsworth.

Hurd, P. D. (Ed.). (1978). *Early adolescence: Perspectives and recommendations.* Washington, DC: U.S. Government Printing Office.

Hurd, P. D. (1984). *Reforming science education: The search for a new vision.* Washington, DC: Council for Basic Education.

Hurd, P. D. (1989a). A life science core for early adolescence. *Middle School Journal, 20*(5), 20–23.

Hurd, P. D. (1989b). Science education and the nation's economy. In A. B. Champagne, B. E. Lovitts, & B. J. Calinger (Eds.), *This year in school science: Scientific literacy.* Washington, DC: American Association for the Advancement of Science.

Hurd, P. D. (1997). *Inventing science education for the new millennium.* New York: Teachers College Press.

Hurd, P. D. (1998, November). What about us? *Middle School Journal, 29*(2), 37–41.

Hurd, P. D. (1999, January). The TIMSS study and science education in the United States. *The Science Teacher.*

Hurd, P. D., Robinson, J. T., McConnell, M. C., & Ross, N. M. (1981). *The status of middle school and junior high school science.* Vol. 1, *Summary Report.* Vol. 2, *Technical Report.* Louisville, CO: Biological Sciences Curriculum Study.

Inhelder, B., & Piaget, J. (1958). *The growth of logical thinking from childhood to adolescence.* New York: Basic Books.

Jasanoff, S., et al. (1997). Conversations with the community: AAAS at the millennium. *Science, 278*(5346), 2066.

Johnson, H. J., & Markle, G. C. (1986). *What research says to the middle school practitioner.* Columbus, OH: National Middle School Association.

Johnson, M. (Ed.). (1980). *Toward adolescence: The middle school years.* The 79th Yearbook for the Study of Education.

Johnson, O. (Ed.). (1994). *Information please almanac.* Boston: Houghton Mifflin.

Katchadourian, H. (1990). "Sexuality." In S. S. Feldman & G. F. Elliott (Eds.), *At the threshold: The developing adolescent.* Cambridge, MA: Harvard University Press.

Kiell, N. (1964). *The universal experience of adolescence.* New York: International Universities.

Kleiman, M. R. R. (1998, Fall). Drugs and drug policy: The case for a slow fix. *Issues, 15,* 1–52.

Kohut, S., Jr. (1980). *The middle school: A bridge between elementary and secondary schools.* Washington, DC: National Education Association.

Koos, L. V. (1920). *The junior high school.* New York: Harcourt, Brace and Howe.

Kozol, J. (1967). *Death at an early age.* Boston: Houghton Mifflin.

Langemann, E. C. (1993). In foreword to R. Takanishi (Ed.), *Adolescence in the 1990s: Risk and opportunity* (p. VII). New York: Teachers College Press.

Levine, D. U., Levine, R. F., & Eubanks, E. E. (1984). Characteristics of effective inner-city intermediate schools. *Phi Delta Kappa, 65*(10).

Lewenstein, B. V. (Ed.). (1992). *When science meets the public.* Washington, DC: American Association for the Advancement of Science.

Lipsitz, J. (1984). *Successful schools for young adolescents.* New Brunswick, NJ: Transaction Books.

Lipsitz, J. (1991, February). "Public policy and young adolescents: A 1990s context for researchers." *Journal of Early Adolescence, 2*(1), 20–27.

Lockheed, M. E., Thorpe, M., Brooks-Gunn, R., Jr., Casserley, P., & Meloon, A. (1985). *Sex and ethnic differences in middle school mathematics, science, and computer science: What do we know?* Princeton, NJ: Educational Testing Service.

Lounsbury, J. H. (Ed.). (1984). *Perspectives: Middle school education, 1964–1984.* Columbus, OH: National Middle School Association.

Malinka, R. (1977). The middle school: Trends and trouble sports. In P. S. George (Ed.), *The middle school: A look ahead.* Fairborn, OH: National Middle School Association.

Manning, M. L. (1993). *Developmentally appropriate middle level schools.* Okney, MD: Association for Childhood Education International.

Marshall, R., & Tucker, M. (1992). *Thinking for a living: Education and the wealth of nations.* New York: Basic Books.

McConnell, M. C. (1981). The middle school: Its philosophy and rationale. In P. D. Hurd, J. T. Robinson, M. C. McConnell, & N. M. Ross, *The status of middle school and junior high school science: Vol. II* (Technical Report). Colorado Springs: Biological Sciences Curriculum Study.

McEwin, C. K., & Clay, R. M. (1983). *A national comparative study of practices and programs of middle and junior high schools.* Boone, NC: Appalachian State University.

McKinsey & Company. (1997). *Connecting K–12 schools to the information highway.* Palo Alto, CA: Author.

Mead, M. (1976). Towards a human science. AAAS Presidential Address. *Science, 19*(903).

Meyer, G. R. (1983). Health education through secondary school biology. (Mimeo). School of Education, Macquarie University, New South Wales.

Moore, K. A. (1992). *National Commission on Children: 1990 survey of parents and children.* Los Altos, CA: Sociometrics Corporation.

Morganett, R. S. (1990). *Skills for living: Group counseling activities for young adolescents.* Champaign, IL: Research Press.

Morrison, W. (1978). *Good schools for middle grade youngsters: Characteristics, practices, and recommendations.* Fairborn, OH: National Middle School Association.

National Academy of Sciences (NAS). (1970). *The life sciences.* Washington, DC: Author.

National Academy of Sciences (NAS). (1993). *Science, technology, and the federal government: National goals for a new era.* Washington, DC: National Academy Press.

National Academy of Sciences. (1996). *The role of scientists in the professional development of science teachers.* Washington, DC: National Academy Press.

National Association of Secondary School Principals. (1960). The junior high school today and tomorrow. *The Bulletin, 44.* Washington, DC: Author.

National Association of Secondary School Principals. (1985). *An agenda for excellence at the middle level.* Reston, VA: Author.

National Board for Professional Teaching Standards. (1996). *Middle childhood/science: Standards for national board certification.* (Draft). Washington, DC: Author.

National Center for Health Statistics. (1996). Hyattsville, MD: Public Health Service.

National Center on Education and the Economy. (1997). *Performance standards: Vol. 2, Middle schools.* Pittsburgh, PA: Author.

National Commission on Teaching and America's Future. (1996). *What matters most: Teaching for America's future.* Woodridge, VA: Author.

National Education Goals Panel. (1991). *The national education goals report: Building a nation of learners.* Washington, DC: U.S. Government Printing Office.

National Institute for Educational Research. (1997). *Teachers, teacher education, and development.* Tokyo: Author.

National Issues Forums. (1997). *Our nation's kids: Is something wrong?* Dubuque, IA: Kendall/Hunt.

National Middle School Association (NMSA). (1982). *This we believe.* Columbus, OH: Author.

National Middle School Association (NMSA). (1986). *Professional certification and preparation for the middle level, a position paper.* Columbus, OH: Author.

National Middle School Association (NMSA). (1995). *This we believe: Developing responsive middle level schools.* Columbus, OH: Author.

National Middle School Association (NMSA). (1997). *A 21st century research agenda: Issues, topics, and questions guiding inquiry into middle level theory and practices.* Columbus, OH: Author.

National Middle School Association. (1998). *Because we believed: A quarter-century of service to young adolescents.* Columbus, OH: Author.

National Research Council (NRC). (1990). *Fulfilling the promise: Biology education in the nation's schools.* Washington, DC: National Academy Press.

National Research Council (NRC). (1993). *Losing generation: Adolescents in high-risk settings.* Washington, DC: National Academy Press.

National Research Council (NRC). (1996a). *Improving America's schools: The role of incentives.* Washington, DC: National Academy Press.

National Research Council (NRC). (1996b). *National science education standards.* Washington, DC: National Academy Press.

National Research Council (NRC). (1997). *Improving teacher preparation and credentialing consistent with the national science education standards: Report of a symposium.* Washington, DC: National Academy Press.

National Research Council (NRC) Committee on Research in Mathematics, Science, and Technology Education. (1985). *Mathematics, science, and technology education: A research agenda.* Washington, DC: National Academy Press.

National Science Foundation (NSF). (1970). *Science education: The task ahead for the National Science Foundation.* (No. 71-13). Washington, DC: Author.

National Science Foundation (NSF). (1986). *Programs for preparation of middle school science and mathematics teachers: Solicitation awards.* Washington, DC: Author.

National Science Foundation (NSF). (1987). *Summary of grants, FY 1984–86.* Washington, DC: Author.

National Science Resources Center. (1998). *Resources for teaching middle school science.* Washington, DC: National Academy Press.

Ochs, V. D. (1981). *Improving practices in middle school science.* 1981 AETS yearbook. Columbus, OH: ERIC Clearinghouse for Science, Mathematics, and Environmental Education.

Olson, L. (1997). *The school to work revolution.* Reading, MA: Addison Wesley.

President's Committee of Advisors on Science and Technology. (1997). *Report to the president on the use of technology to strengthen K–12 education in the United States.* Washington, DC: Author.

Public Agenda. (1997). *Our nation's kids: Is something wrong?* Dubuque, IA: Kendall/Hunt.

Reinhartz, J., & Beach, D. M. (1983). *Improving middle school instruction: A research based self-assessment system.* Washington, DC: National Education Association.

Report of the Superintendents' Middle Grades Task Force. (1987). *Caught in the middle: Educational reform for young adolescents in California public schools.* Sacramento, CA: Bureau of Publications.

Robinson, S. F. (1997). *Building knowledge for a nation of learners: A framework for education research.* Washington, DC: Government Printing Office.

Rockefeller Brothers Fund. (1958). *The pursuit of excellence: Education and the future of America.* Garden City, NY: Doubleday.

Saskatchewan Newstart, Inc. (1972). *Life skills: A course in applied problem solving.* Prince Albert, Saskatchewan: Author.

SCANS. (1992). *Skills and tasks for jobs: A SCANS report for America 2000.* Washington, DC: U.S. Department of Labor.

Silberman, C. E. (1970). *Crisis in the classroom.* New York: Random House.

Spencer, H. (1860). *Education: Intellectual, mind, and physical.* New York: John B. Alden.

Standing Committee on Teacher Education (1983, September). Recommended standards for the preparation and certification of teachers of science at the middle junior high school level. *Science and Children, 21.*

Takanishi, R. (Ed.). (1993). *Adolescence in the 1990s: Risk and opportunity.* New York: Teachers College Press.

Tanner, J. M. (1971). Sequence, tempo, and individual variation in the growth and development of boys and girls aged twelve to sixteen. *Daedalus, 100*(4), 909–930.

Thayer, V. T. (Chairman). (1937). *Science in general education.* New York: D. Appleton-Century.

The third branch of science debits. (1992). *Science, 256*(5 053), 44–62.

Thorndike, E. L. (1907). *The elimination of pupils from school.* Washington, DC: U.S. Bureau of Education. (Bulletin No. 4).

Toepfer, C. F., Jr. (1977). The middle school as a multiple school: A means for survival. In P. S. George (Ed.), *The middle school: A look ahead.* Fairborn, OH: National Middle School Association.

Treacy, J. B. (1968). What is the middle school? *Catholic School Journal, 68,* 56–58.

Turner et al. (1998, May 8). Adolescent sexual behavior, drug use, and violence: Increased reporting with computer survey technology. *Science, 280,* 867–873.

Tye, K. A. (1985). *The junior high school in search of a mission.* Lanham, MD: University Press of America.

UNESCO (n.d.). *Health education and biology teaching.* Paris: Author.

U.S. Bureau of the Census. (1993). (113th Edition). Washington, DC: Author.

U.S. Bureau of the Census. (1994). *Household and family characteristics, March 1994.* Washington, DC: Author.

U.S. Congress, House Committee on Science. (1998). *Unlocking our future: Toward a new national science policy.* Washington, DC: Author. http://www.house. gov/science/science-policy-report. htm, p. 11.

U.S. Department of Education. (1996). *Getting America's students ready for the 21st century: Meeting the technology literacy challenge.* Washington, DC: Author.

U.S. Department of Education. (1997). *Building knowledge for a nation of learners: A framework for education research, 1997.* Washington, DC: Author.

University of Southern California and Sutherland Learning Associates, Incorporated. (1979). *Science education for early adolescents: A needs assessment and flexibility study.* Final report to the Alfred P. Sloan Foundation. Los Angeles, CA: Author.

Van Til, W., Vars, G. S., & Lounsbury, J. (1967). *Modern education for the junior high years.* New York: Bobbs-Merrill.

Ventura, S. J., et al. (1997). *Teenage births in the United States: National and state trends, 1990–1996.* Hyattsville, MD: National Center for Health Statistics.

Walton, J. F. (1973). *A report on measurement and the quality of life.* Washington, DC: U.S. Department of Health, Education, and Welfare.

Weiss, I. R. (1980). *Developing options for managing NSF's middle school science education programs.* (3 vols.: *Executive Summary, Final Report,* and *Appendix.*) Research Triangle Park, NC: Research Triangle Institute.

Whitaker, C. M., & Bastian, L. D. (1991). *Teenage victims: A national crime survey report.* Washington, DC: U.S. Department of Justice.

Wiles, J. W., & Bondi, J. (1986a). *The essential middle school.* Tampa, FL: Wiles, Bondi, and Associates.

Wiles, J. W., & Bondi, J. (1986b). *What research says to the middle school practitioner.* Columbus, OH: Association for Supervision and Curriculum Development.

Wilkinson, J. J. G. (1847). *Science for all.* London: William Newberry.

Wirth, A. G. (1992). *Education and work for the year 2000: Choices we face.* San Francisco: Jossey-Bass.

World Health Organization (WHO). (1978, September). *Primary health care: A report of the International Conference on Primary Health Care.* Alma-Ata: Author.

Index

About the Author

Paul DeHart Hurd is a Professor Emeritus in the School of Education, Stanford University. He is a specialist in science education and has had 18 years of experience in teaching science in the middle grades. At Stanford University he was in charge of teacher education for the middle grades and high school. In 1998 the National Middle School Association established the Paul DeHart Hurd Yearly Award of $1,000 to honor an outstanding middle school educator.

He received his EdD in science education from Stanford University in 1949. He holds honorary Doctor of Science degrees from the University of Northern Colorado, 1980; Ball State University, 1979; and Drake University, 1974. His research has focused on the history of science curriculum reform movements in the United States and foreign countries. He is the author of nine books and monographs and some 300 published articles on science education.

He is a fellow of the American Association for the Advancement of Science.